Ancient Nubia

A Captivating Guide to One of the Earliest Civilizations in Africa and African Kingdoms, Such as the Kingdoms of Kerma and Kush

© Copyright 2021

All Rights Reserved. No part of this book may be reproduced in any form without permission in writing from the author. Reviewers may quote brief passages in reviews.

Disclaimer: No part of this publication may be reproduced or transmitted in any form or by any means, mechanical or electronic, including photocopying or recording, or by any information storage and retrieval system, or transmitted by email without permission in writing from the publisher.

While all attempts have been made to verify the information provided in this publication, neither the author nor the publisher assumes any responsibility for errors, omissions or contrary interpretations of the subject matter herein.

This book is for entertainment purposes only. The views expressed are those of the author alone, and should not be taken as expert instruction or commands. The reader is responsible for his or her own actions.

Adherence to all applicable laws and regulations, including international, federal, state and local laws governing professional licensing, business practices, advertising and all other aspects of doing business in the US, Canada, UK or any other jurisdiction is the sole responsibility of the purchaser or reader.

Neither the author nor the publisher assumes any responsibility or liability whatsoever on the behalf of the purchaser or reader of these materials. Any perceived slight of any individual or organization is purely unintentional.

Free Bonus from Captivating History (Available for a Limited time)

Hi History Lovers!

Now you have a chance to join our exclusive history list so you can get your first history ebook for free as well as discounts and a potential to get more history books for free! Simply visit the link below to join.

Captivatinghistory.com/ebook

Also, make sure to follow us on Facebook, Twitter and Youtube by searching for Captivating History.

Contents

INTRODUCTION - THE SECRETS BENEATH 1

CHAPTER 1 - THE DOMAINS OF FORGOTTEN KINGDOMS 7
    The Geography and Boundaries of Ancient Nubia 7
    The Cataracts 10
    Entering Nubia from the North 13

CHAPTER 2 - LOWER, MIDDLE, AND UPPER NUBIA: AN OVERVIEW 16
    The Divisions of Lower, Middle, and Upper Nubia 16
    Lower Nubia 17
    Middle Nubia 19
    Upper Nubia 22

CHAPTER 3 - THE PREHISTORIC CULTURES OF ANCIENT NUBIA 31
    The Mysterious Prehistoric Civilization of Nabta Playa 33
    Early Khartoum (circa 5000 BCE) 44
    The Rise and Fall of the A- and B-Group Cultures in Prehistoric Nubia (3800-3100 BCE) 47
    C-Group Culture (circa 2400-1550 BCE) 55
    The Medjay (1800-1500 BCE) 60
    Pre-Kerma & Early Kerma Cultures 62

CHAPTER 4 - THE RISE AND FALL OF THE MIDDLE AND CLASSIC KERMA CULTURES 65
    Middle and Early-Classic Kerma, Center of the Early Kushite Kingdom 66

Classic Kerma - The Golden Age 78
The Fall of Kerma 83
CHAPTER 5 - THE KINGDOM OF KUSH 88
Rising from the Ashes of Conquest 88
Napata 90
From Kingdom to Empire: Kush Rises Again 96
Meroe 109
CHAPTER 6 - THE PYRAMIDS OF ANCIENT NUBIA 121
CONCLUSION - THE MYSTERY IN THE SANDS 131
FREE BONUS FROM CAPTIVATING HISTORY (AVAILABLE FOR A LIMITED TIME) 134
HERE'S ANOTHER BOOK BY CAPTIVATING HISTORY THAT YOU MIGHT LIKE 135

Introduction – The Secrets Beneath

The morning sun awakens and rises over a rock-strewn and rugged desert, painting the desolate landscape with an already searing glow. Only a slight jingle and the bray of sheep disturbs the silence while a shepherd drives his flock of sheep through the dawn's hazy heat. Long shadows stretch across the desert floor as the sun-kissed stones of dozens of ancient pyramids rebuff the sun's ferocious light, just as they have done for over three thousand years.

Appearing as the points of arrowheads jutting from the desert floor and piercing the deep blue sky, the sight of the silent pyramids upon the desolate plain is both jarring and offsetting. Whispering of the might and power of an advanced civilization that has long gone quiet, the pyramids stand as silent sentinels in the morning sun, the reminder of a once thriving and flourishing culture whose secrets still lay silent in the shifting sands below.

If one did not know better, one would believe this scene to be a description of the landscapes of Egypt, the technologically advanced ancient empire and culture that has dominated the minds and imaginations of millions of souls over the last millennia.

But one would be wrong.

This is not Egypt.

This is northern Sudan, home to ancient Nubia, whose various cultures rivaled the world's greatest empires and whose Kingdom of Kush brought even mighty Egypt to its knees.

The sprawling collection of pyramids, now sitting alone atop a windswept desert plain, mark the once thriving city of Meroe, which was the home to a civilization that played a major role in the histories of northwest Africa and the Mediterranean.

A place that has been all but forgotten to most modern minds.

For over two thousand years, Egypt and Nubia shared their gods, art, architecture, and trade goods. Their people groups intermarried, created political partnerships with one another, served in each other's armies, fought with another, and fought against each other. Nubians served as pharaohs in Egypt, and Egyptians held positions in the Kushite kingdoms. Their empires and dynasties rose and fell and then rose and fell again, an ebb and flow that matched the rise and fall of the Nile River, which brought life to them both.

The Kerma and Kush kingdoms of ancient Nubia, which were descended from ancient African civilizations, controlled massive networks of trade and commerce routes along the Nile, the Red Sea, and into eastern Africa. Nubia, whose very name was synonymous with "gold," was rich in resources such as gold, onyx, carnelian, and other precious metals, as well as incense, ivory, copper, and iron ore.

The pyramids of the Nubian empires outnumbered those of Egypt nearly two to one. Nubian palaces, artwork, tombs, and burial customs were shared with that of Egypt yet displayed their own distinct flair. Nubia's innovatively crafted and jeweled adornments were famous throughout the world, with her craftspeople drawing from metalworking techniques that would not be rediscovered in Europe for another thousand years. Its pottery and handblown glass were desired by civilizations in Greece and Israel, and Nubia's religious amulets have been found as far away as modern Afghanistan.

The armies of the kingdoms of ancient Nubia were ferocious in battle, and its soldiers were craved as mercenaries. The mercenary soldiers of Nubian armies helped Egypt become a mighty military power, assisting in expelling the Hyksos during Egypt's Eighteenth Dynasty while also putting down the rebellions of their own people, thus establishing a period of unprecedented growth for their northern neighbor. Called "Ta-Seti," meaning "the Land of the Bow," the armies of Nubia were known for their archers who faced the ferocious Assyrian Empire in 674 BCE, handing its famed military one of its worst defeats.[1,2] Almost seven hundred years later, the ruling queens of ancient Kush, called Kandakes (also Candaces or Kentakes), went toe to toe with the forces of Rome, even when the Roman armies crushed those of neighboring Egypt.

After a series of invasions and incursions against one another along their northern border with Egypt and even after Rome annihilated the northern army of Kush at Napata, the rulers of Kush would not give in. With brutal fury, the Kushite armies retaliated against the dangerous Roman prefect Publius Petronius, the governor of Egypt, and battled his armies to a standstill. Unable or unwilling to expend more resources against the fierce armies of Kush, Petronius acquiesced to a trade agreement with the Nubian empire, establishing centuries of favorable trade with the Kushite kingdom.[3]

The kingdoms and empires of ancient Nubia stood for over six thousand years, carving a significant role into the histories of some of the world's mightiest cultures. Its achievements rivaled that of Egypt and other powers of the Mediterranean, and its archaeological remains are still scattered throughout southern Egypt and Sudan.

---

[1] Jarus, Owen (2017). "Ancient Nubia, A Brief History." Live Science. 9 June 2021. https://www.livescience.com/57875-ancient-nubia.html.

[2] Eph'al, Israel (2005). "Esarhaddon, Egypt, and Shubria: Politics and Propaganda." *Journal of Cuneiform Studies*. University of Chicago Press. p 57.

[3] Fluehr-Lobban, Carolyn; Rhodes, Kharyssa. (2004). *Race and Identity in the Nile Valley: Ancient and Modern Perspectives.* The Red Sea Press. p 55.

But the questions remain—for a civilization responsible for so much, why is so little known about ancient Nubia? Why are its crowning achievements not mentioned in the same breath as those of Egypt? For a civilization whose proud descendants still exist, eat, work, and reside along the life-giving Nile River, why is the landscape of ancient Nubia not swarmed with archaeological digs and excavations like its neighbor to the north? Why does the world not wait with bated breath to see what lies beneath the shifting and mysterious desert sands of northern Sudan as it does for new historical discoveries in Egypt, Israel, or Turkey? Why has its own written languages remained shrouded in mystery, still not fully understood after thousands of years? And why has modern archaeology shied away from the powerful influence of ancient Nubia upon Egyptian culture and trade throughout the Mediterranean?

Why has the modern mind forgotten such an important culture, whose very existence made so much of the Mediterranean and African cultures possible?

This book is a journey of discovery of ancient Nubia. It is a guide to one of the earliest civilizations of not just Africa but of the world. And through a survey of Nubia's known history, including a deep examination of its Kerma and Kushite kingdoms, it will seek to illuminate the answers to the question of why such a mighty civilization has been all but forgotten.

The mystery of ancient Nubia swirls in the sands that shift about its ruined palaces, tombs, and pyramids. The stones of its intimidating and massive structures stand as silent sentinels in the evening sun, casting long shadows upon the desert floor. But if one looks carefully beneath the surface, one can still hear the thrum and energy of a powerful kingdom from long ago, a kingdom whose secrets still wait to be discovered by those with the courage and the curiosity to look beyond the surface and dig deep into the sands.

Chapter 1 – The Domains of Forgotten Kingdoms

The Geography and Boundaries of Ancient Nubia

The area commonly referred to as ancient Nubia was located upon the Nile River and lay immediately south of classical Upper Egypt. In fact, what was northern Nubia is now part of southern Egypt, with the rest of the former civilization making up modern-day Sudan.

Observing ancient Nubia from the clouds above, it is easiest to imagine a desert landscape with a blue scar, a curved strip of blue ribbon in the shape of a lower consonant -*n*- which marks the Nile River. Slight, thin pockets of green shade away from the blue, interspersed sporadically between gravel and stone expanses, overshadowed with swirling sands that lap against gray granite.

Over a span of 300,000 years, humanity has moved and shifted along this blue ribbon that arrogantly cuts through the otherwise brown and gray topography of the Nubian and Libyan Deserts. Eight thousand years ago, nomadic cattle herders called this region home, creating religious cults dedicated to cattle gods, homes, and some of the oldest known pottery in the world's history. Seven thousand years ago, settlers began to domesticate sheep and goats and created rock wall paintings of men and women hunting wild animals with bows and arrows.

This mysterious culture is believed to be responsible for the megalithic monuments at Nabta Playa, an astronomical achievement that potentially predates Stonehenge by 2,000 years and the pyramids of Egypt by 2,500 years.[4] Evidence suggests these massive stone blocks were moved into place by people who understood the complex motion of constellational alignments and the movement of the sun and moon across the sky. They were semi-agrarian, domesticating sorghum and millet. Five thousand five hundred years ago, the first evidence of complex agriculture appeared, with early Nubians likely using ox-driven waterwheels to irrigate the dry land, producing grass seeds, roots and tubers, early legumes, and fruits.[5] And 4,500 years ago, mankind began to erect kingdoms that rose, toppled, and rose and toppled again near the life-giving sustenance of the Nile, giving birth to the eventual civilizations of Kerma and Kush.

In the work *Nubia: Corridor to Africa*, Cambridge historian William Y. Adams wrote that Nubia was "the corridor which men, things, and ideas passed from one world to another."[6] Nubia was not a backwater slum or the wild frontier. Nubia was a thriving civilization with a complex and ever-evolving relationship with surrounding empires, cities, and sovereign states.

---

[4] Betz, Eric. (2020). "Nabta Playa: The World's First Astronomical Site Was Built in Africa and Is Older Than Stonehenge." *Discover Magazine*. 9 June 2021. https://www.discovermagazine.com/the-sciences/nabta-playa-the-worlds-first-astronomical-site-was-built-in-africa-and-is.

[5] Svitil, Kathy. (1994). "What the Nubians Ate." *Discover Magazine*. 9 June 2021. https://www.discovermagazine.com/the-sciences/what-the-nubians-ate.

[6] Adams, William Y. (1977). *Nubia: Corridor to Africa*. Princeton University Press. p 20.

The Cataracts

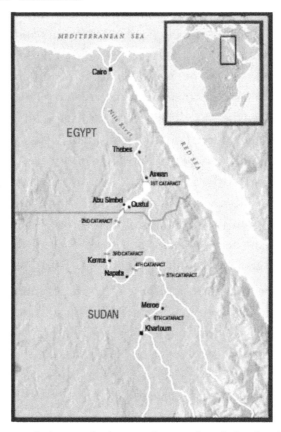

To understand the evolution and growth of the lands of ancient Nubia, one must understand the evolution and flow of the Nile River and its cataracts, which geographically defined the cultures and movements that resided along its shores.

Traveling south along the Nile River (which is upstream, as the Nile River flows south to north, traveling about 6,650 kilometers—about 4,100 miles—from the higher elevation of Lake Victoria in modern-day Uganda, Kenya, and Tanzania up through northeast Africa to the Nile Delta), the Nubian region began south of modern-day Aswan and fifty miles north of Khartoum, where the Blue and White Nile join together as they carve their way down breathtaking granite canyons.

While the Nile River linked Nubia and Egypt together, it also provided a natural defense between the two regions. Near Aswan was what was known as the First Cataract of the Nile (from the Greek word καταρρέω, meaning "to flow down"). In truth, what was called the First Cataract was actually the sixth cataract of the Nile, with the first five cataracts moving south to north and lying within ancient Nubia. But as the reader will see, much of what we know of ancient Nubia comes from Egyptian and Greek perspectives, and since these civilizations moved north to south, the final cataract of the Nile was, to them, the first.

The Cataracts of the Nile were areas of the Nile River that are often narrow and rocky, impeding river travel due to the potential ferocity and unpredictability of the waters. Depending upon the annual flooding of the Nile River, the water could range from easy flowing to raging whitewater, and it could switch between the two quickly and unexpectedly. Underneath the surface of the waters of the cataracts were jutting granite stones that rose from the softer sandstone beneath, making river travel through the cataracts uncertain and potentially deadly to ships and travelers.

The First Cataract, laying south of Aswan, is now the site of the Aswan Low Dam, which was built in 1902, the first dam built across the Nile. However, in ancient times, Aswan was known as the ancient city of Swenett (Syene) and was a frontier town upon the border of Egypt and the Nubian kingdoms to the south.

Swenett was located on the east side of the river, and from Swenett, one could travel unimpeded north along the river to the Nile Delta, thus allowing goods and services to extend easily from Swenett to the Mediterranean Sea. The city of Swenett was dedicated to the antelope-horned goddess Setet, the goddess of the Nile and of the bow, who was worshiped at nearby Elephantine Island. Setet was also worshiped as a goddess of childbirth, as the Egyptians believed their portion of the Nile was birthed at Swenett; thus, this is where their kingdom began.[7] Due to the abundance of granite (called syenite) in the area, this was also where the kingdoms of Egypt mined their stone for their massive building projects and for trade. The Nile River made northern transport possible for the massive amounts of stone they quarried over the thousands of years, providing granite for not only their kingdom but also for others via trade.

Every dynasty of ancient Egypt equipped Swenett with a large military garrison. Truth be told, Swenett was a military town that stood opposite nearby Elephantine, which was considered the sacred spring of the Nile River by the Egyptians; it was home to the gods Khnum, Heqet, and Setet. Also nearby was the island of Philae; its massive temple complex was the home of the thriving cult of Isis. Ships that were skilled enough to pass north or south through the First Cataract were subject to the ancients' equivalent of tolls, custom charges, and inspections. As such, the Nubians symbolized the town of Swenett with the symbol for "market," as this was one of their primary entry points for trade with the Egyptian world. This region was also considered of prime importance during Egypt's Roman occupation and was a launching point for both Rome's and Nubia's military incursions against one another.[8]

---

[7] Hill, J. (2008). "Satet." Ancient Egypt Online. 9 June 2021. https://ancientegyptonline.co.uk/satet/.

[8] Robinson, Arthur R. (1928). "The Arab Dynasty of Dar For (Darfur): Part 2." *Journal of the Royal African Society* XXVIII. p 55-67.

Swenett's purpose and importance, and thus the First Cataract's importance, was mentioned in many ancient documents by writers such as Pliny the Elder, Stephanus of Byzantium, Herodotus, Ptolemy, and Strabo. Historians suggest that this region was referred to in the Hebrew Tanakh, particularly the Books of Ezekiel and Isaiah.

The Second to the Third Cataract traditionally defines what some scholars argue as Middle Nubia, which consisted of an arid, rocky desert similar to that of Lower Nubia, but it was also the home of Sai Island, which was used as a major necropolis of the Upper Nubian Kerma culture. Sai Island was a strategic fortification used by invading militaries and the Kushite kingdom. It was the location of a medieval cathedral and even an Ottoman fortress. During the Eighteenth Dynasty of Egypt, the Third Cataract was the dividing line between the Egyptian empire and the kingdom of ancient Nubia.

Upper Nubia was defined as the area from the Third Cataract to the Sixth Cataract upriver, where the white and blue waters of the Nile coalesced. This is the area that was widely known as the home of the archaeologically rich kingdoms of Kerma and Kush. Still considered desert lands, the area between the Third and Sixth Cataracts was more conducive to life and rainfall, and it was more accessible via trade, thus the creation of long-lasting civilizations and kingdoms.

Entering Nubia from the North

Traveling directionally south upon the Nile from Swenett (or upriver, as the Nile flows south to north), one enters the land of the ancient Nubians, whose lands contrasted sharply with that of their northern neighbor.

One of the primary differences between the Nubian and Egyptian kingdoms was directly caused by the geography that affected the Nile. While the banks of the Nile in Egypt were marked with lush grasses and fertile fields created by the Nile's annual flooding, the Nile River of ancient Nubia was much different and was referred to in several ancient sources as the "Cataract Nile."

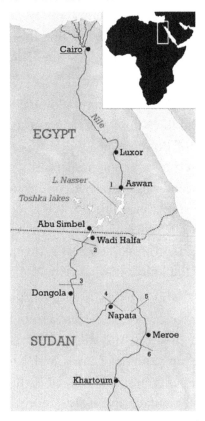

Due to the geographical positioning of Nubia's five cataracts and the granite outcroppings that rose from the sandstone beneath, large fertile plains did not extend outward from the Nile as they did in Egypt, making irrigation and agriculture much more difficult, particularly in Lower Nubia, which lay to the north and received less than four total inches of rainfall per year (like ancient Egypt, Nubia was subdivided into separate areas that reflected the flow of the Nile River). Combined with the arid desert and extreme lack of rainfall, the lands of what we now refer to as Lower Nubia could not sustain the massive field growth that so marked Egypt to the north and Upper

Nubia to the south, which received upward of forty inches of rain per year.[9]

What did mark the lands of Lower and Middle Nubia was its abundance of gold and deposits of precious metals that were naturally placed by the evolution of the Nile River over billions of years between the river's cataracts, enabling the kingdoms of ancient Nubia to trade precious metals for grain and other commodities with its neighbors, particularly Egypt. This also created a natural barrier and defense against invading armies, as invaders could not sustain their forces long-term due to the lack of available food and resources.

While the Nile River maintained a somewhat straight line throughout Egypt, in Nubia, the Nile moved through a series of bends and cuts that created unique waypoints, strategic markers, and defensible positions for the Nubian kingdoms. The Greek geographer and mathematician Eratosthenes gave one of the most accurate descriptions of the Nile as it moved south to north through these points, writing in circa 240 BCE, that "It [the Nile] has a similar shape to a backwards letter -n-. It flows northward from Meroe about 2700 stadia [eight stadia equals one Roman mile (five thousand feet)], then turns back to the south and the winter sunset for about 3700 stadia, and it almost reaches the same parallel as the Meroe region and makes its way far into Libya. Then it makes another turn, and flows northward 5300 stadia to the great cataract, curving slightly to the east; then 1200 stadia to the smaller cataract at Syene [Swenett] and then 5300 more to the sea."[10]

---

[9] (2009). "Sudan – Climate." Nations Encyclopedia. 10 June 2021. https://www.nationsencyclopedia.com/Africa/Sudan-CLIMATE.html.

[10] Jones, H.L. (1932). *The Geography, Volume VIII.* Harvard University Press. https://penelope.uchicago.edu/Thayer/E/Roman/Texts/Strabo/17A1*.html.

Chapter 2 – Lower, Middle, and Upper Nubia: An Overview

The Divisions of Lower, Middle, and Upper Nubia

While Egypt lay to the north, Nubia's eastern boundary was bordered by the harsh Libyan Desert. Unlike the Libyan Desert, the Nubian Desert is made up of rocky terrain with granite outcroppings and rugged sandstone, and while large sand dunes exist, they are much less common than what one typically tends to think of when imagining the desert.

The western border of ancient Nubia ended at the desolate Red Sea Hills, which rise over seven thousand feet above sea level at modern-day Jabal Erba before descending to the Red Sea, an essential waterway of trade throughout the ancient world, moving spices, silk, and exotic hardwood from the lands of Punt and Arabia.[11]

---

[11] Kotarba-Morley, Anna M. (2018). "Ancient Ports of Trade on the Red Sea Coasts—The 'Parameters of Attractiveness' of Site Locations and Human Adaptations to Fluctuating Land- and Sea-Scapes. Case Study Berenike Troglodytica, Southeastern Egypt." Geological Setting, Palaeoenvironment and Archaeology of the Red Sea. p 741 – 774. 10 June 2021. https://link.springer.com/chapter/10.1007/978-3-319-99408-6_34.

Unlike Egypt, whose Lower and Upper regions were distinguished by the vein-like Nile River Delta and the river proper, respectively, Nubia was subdivided into two to three regions, dependent upon its timeline, historical reference—Lower, Middle, and Upper—and the cataracts (for general purposes, Nubia is most often referred to as either Lower or Upper Nubia).

Lower Nubia

Lower Nubia traditionally has been recognized as bordering Egypt to the north at the First Cataract of ancient Swenett and moving upriver to the Second Cataract, referred to as the Great Cataract. Located six miles north of the modern city of Wadi Halfa, the Great Cataract is now submerged under Lake Nassar.[12] Called Wawat by the ancient Egyptians, Lower Nubia was home to some of the world's most ancient cultures, and archaeological evidence exists that suggests that this part of Nubia was fertile grassland as recently as five thousand years ago.[13] (This region, like much of the area of Saharan Africa, is theorized to move between dry and wet climates over a 41,000-year cycle, where the tilt of the Earth shifts between 22 degrees and 24.5 degrees due to the Earth's precession. Precession is the third movement of the Earth other than daily rotations and annual revolutions around the sun, where the Earth's axis essentially shifts the equinoxes due to the gravitational pull of the sun and moon. This phenomenon is believed to have a massive effect upon the path of the North African monsoon, pushing it southward and bringing with it heavy rains and thus extensive vegetation growth. As the Sahara

---

[12] "Cataracts of the Nile." 10 June 2021.

https://web.archive.org/web/20100217042412/http://fummo.com/info/Cataracts_of_the_Nile.html.

[13] Houérou, Henry N. (2008). *Bioclimatology and Biogeography of Africa*. Springer Science & Business Media. p 16.

Desert of Africa is currently locked in a dry cycle, if this theory holds true, the Sahara Desert will again be green in 17,000 CE.[14])

Exploited and occupied by Egypt during its Middle Kingdom period (2030–1650 BCE) due to its massive precious metal deposits, the terrain of Lower Nubia was hotly contested by the Kerma people of Upper Nubia, with the Kingdom of Kerma performing incursions into the Egyptian territory throughout its existence. After finally retaking Lower Nubia from Egyptian control around 1700 BCE, Lower Nubia fell into the hands of the Kingdom of Kerma to the south. But by the New Kingdom period of ancient Egypt, all of Nubia had been assimilated into the Egyptian empire. During Egypt's one-hundred-year Second Intermediate Period, beginning in 1650 BCE, the Lower Nubian city of Napata briefly became the capital of Kush before the capital shifted farther south to the more easily defensible island of Meroe.[15]

After the Kingdom of Kush dissolved in 350 CE, ancient Nubia became part of what has been titled the Ballana culture, a culture that built large earthen mounds as tombs that consisted of sacrifices and elaborate burial customs. The Greeks called this otherwise mysterious group the Noubadians (referred to in this book as Nobataes), and they were ruled by a king known as Silko.[16]

By the 5th century and with the introduction of Christianity, the deserts of Lower Nubia became Christianized as part of the Kingdom of Makuria. They were heavily influenced by the nearby bishop's see on the Island of Sai (between the Third and Fourth Cataracts of the Nile) but quickly gave way to Islamification at the turn of the millennium.

---

[14] Gregerson, Erik. (2019). "Precession of the Equinoxes." Britannica. 10 June 2021. https://www.britannica.com/science/precession-of-the-equinoxes.

[15] (2021). "Lower Nubia." Wikipedia. 10 June 2021. https://en.wikipedia.org/wiki/Lower_Nubia.

[16] (2020). "X-Group Culture." Oriental Institute, The University of Chicago. 11 June 2021. https://oi.uchicago.edu/museum-exhibits/nubia/x-group-culture.

Under Arabic control, Lower Nubia was first overseen by the brother of Saladin, Turan-Shah, and was considered of major strategic importance in moving south along the Nile. Over the next three centuries, Lower Nubia was a point of contention between Muslim and Christian kings until it was eventually overrun by the Funj Sultanate in 1504, the sultanate considered "an African-Nubian empire with a Muslim façade."[17] As Egypt was appropriated by the Ottoman Empire in 1517, Lower and Middle Nubia were absorbed into the conquest as well and has remained primarily under Egyptian control since.

Middle Nubia

When classifying Middle Nubia separately from Lower and Upper Nubia, scholars agree that Middle Nubia lay between the Great Cataract and the Third Cataract, presently called the Abri-Delgo Reach.

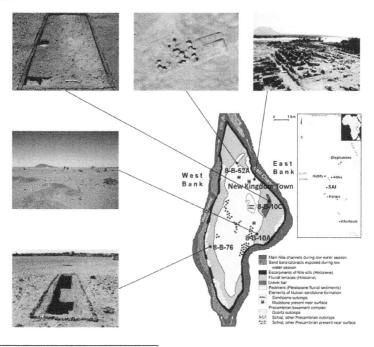

---

[17] Loimeier, Roman (2013). *Muslim Societies in Africa: A Historical Anthropology.* Indiana University. p 141.

Middle Nubia's most well-known feature was Sai Island, a rather large island centered in the Nile River measuring over seven miles long and three miles wide. Sai Island, which was settled by Paleolithic peoples over ten thousand years ago, alternated as a possession of the Nubian Kingdoms of Kerma and Kush and as an outpost of the Egyptian empires of the New Kingdom (1520-1075 BCE), the Makurians (831-1365 CE), and the Ottomans (1580-1823) before falling to the kingdom and then the country of Egypt.

Sai Island is an archaeological treasure trove. Evidence exists that Sai was used by the Kerma culture as a necropolis. Elaborate tomb monuments still stand in the area, and extant funerary artwork, jewelry, and remains confirm that Sai Island was the home of complex ceremonies and religious work. Evidence suggests that Sai Island was a major fixture of the mid- and late Kerma culture, and even ancient Egyptian documents suggest a high degree of honor for this area of ancient Nubia, naming the island Shaat.

During the New Kingdom, Middle Nubia was a province of Egypt, and Sai Island demonstrates a great deal of evidence that confirms its occupation and strategic importance in holding Lower and Middle Nubia. On the eastern side of Sai Island, the remains of a large fortified and defensible walled village attest to the building of a garrison outpost. A temple dedicated to the Egyptian sun god Amun stood in the center of the town, and two cemeteries canvassed with pyramid structures (dated to the New Kingdom period as well) lay just to the outside. Evidence suggests that the village was refurbished multiple times over its history, leading to the belief that the fortification was highly valued over the centuries. Additionally, cemeteries designed and built during the Meroitic period of the Kingdom of Kush (300 BCE-400 CE) lay to the north, again confirming Sai Island's extended use as a sacred burial site.

Burial grounds dated to the Middle Ages suggest that a large Christian cathedral and other medieval settlements were built upon Sai Island, with several scholars believing that Sai Island was a dedicated bishop's residence. This further affirms that this area of Middle Nubia was considered a place of strategic power over the surrounding countryside.

As the Ottoman Empire continued to expand its hold upon northeastern Africa after conquering Egypt, in 1582, the Ottoman army advanced along the Nile to take Nubia. After taking Sai Island, the Ottomans desired to move farther south to lay claim to Upper Nubia, craving its trade resources and capabilities. At Atshaw Hannek (opposite Tombos), the Funj army, who had lost Lower Nubia to the Ottomans years prior, rose up to meet the Ottoman incursion. After battling to a stalemate, the Ottoman army retreated to Sai Island and built a large fortress called Qalat Sai atop the earlier Egyptian New Kingdom settlement. The Funj Sultanate installed garrisons south of Atshaw Hannek, ceasing the southern spread of the Ottoman empire until 1823.[18]

---

[18] Peacock, A.C.S. (2012). "The Ottomans and the Funj sultanate in the sixteenth and seventeenth centuries." *Bulletin of the School of Oriental and African Studies.* University of London. Vol 75 p 87-111.

Upper Nubia

When divided into Lower, Middle, and Upper, Upper Nubia was typically considered beginning near the Third Cataract and running to the Sixth Cataract, where the Atbara River and the Nile River come together. However, most historians, when referring to Upper Nubia post 1700 BCE, refers to Upper Nubia as from the Second Cataract to the Shendi Reach.

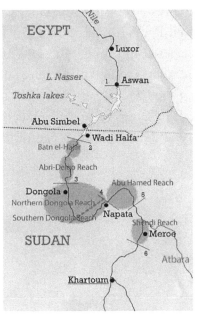

Upper Nubia lay at a higher elevation than Lower Nubia, receiving considerably more rainfall than its lower counterpart. Five thousand years ago, Upper Nubia was much more conducive to agriculture and could support larger, more permanent settlements. While Lower Nubia was arguably filled with larger gold and precious mineral deposits, Upper Nubia was more centralized, allowing the region to become a major trade center, controlling the trade routes from Egypt into lower Africa and from Libya to the Red Sea. This enabled Upper Nubia to accumulate massive amounts of wealth, and it became the home of an empire that would challenge ancient Egypt's domination of northeast Africa.

During ancient Nubia's prehistoric period, the Nubian culture was primarily nomadic and semi-pastoral, traversing and setting up small settlements throughout Lower Nubia. However, in approximately 3500 BCE, several permanent settlements began to appear in Upper Nubia to the south. DNA and dental analysis of remains throughout Upper Nubia shows that many of these early settlers were similar to those of Lower Nubia but also shared characteristics of sub-Saharan people groups, indicating an intermingling of cultures. Pottery shards indicate knowledge of Lower Nubian ceramic making, even though the pottery of Upper Nubia was distinct in shape and appearance. This culture would come to be known as the Pre-Kerma culture.[19]

Kerma

Due to the natural buffer created by the terrain of Lower Nubia, Upper Nubia's villages and cities began to grow and thrive outside of the direct control of Egypt. The soil of Upper Nubia was more conducive to crop growth. Planned cities and villages began to rise, and by 2600 BCE, the city of Kerma had grown into a regional power. It was home to over two thousand people, and it had palaces, temples, homes, and storage areas for seed, harvested food, and animals.

Referred to as the Kushites by the Egyptian pharaohs, the Middle Kerma people were primarily agrarian, trading raised goods such as grains, fruits, and livestock within the metropolitan city walls of Kerma and Sai. Markets that traded in ceramic and metal-worked goods (jewelry, tools, and weapons) were common, and evidence suggests that taxes and tolls were levied by administrators and traders throughout the kingdom.

By 1700 BCE, the city of Kerma was home to over ten thousand people and had consolidated power between the Third and Sixth Cataracts. With a highly efficient military, Kerma performed regular

---

[19] "Sudan, Egypt, and Nubia Prehistory – AD 1000s The Raymond and Beverly Sackler Gallery." The British Museum. 15 June 2021. https://www.britishmuseum.org/collection/galleries/sudan-egypt-and-nubia.

incursions along Egypt's southern border at the Second Cataract, prompting Egypt to build thirteen fortifications to protect its assets, such as gold and granite mines, that they had seized in Lower Nubia in the prior three centuries.

During Egypt's Thirteenth Dynasty (1803-1649 BCE), Egypt's power structure became destabilized, and by 1640, it had devolved into multiple dynasties fighting for control of a shattered empire. Seizing the opportunity of Egypt's weakened government, Kerma began to successfully perform raids along Lower Nubia.[20]

By 1700, most of Lower Nubia was controlled by Kerma, which enabled the Kermite civilization to move into what is known as the Classic Kerma phase (circa 1750-1550 BCE). The influx of gold, precious metals, and copper from Lower Nubia enabled Kerma's power to surge, beginning a massive building phase throughout what was now becoming the Kushite empire.

Kush

During the Classic Kerma phase, Kerma aligned with Salitis the Hyksos, who had established his own dominant rule within the

---

[20] Edwards, David. (2004). *The Nubian Past: An Archaeology of the Sudan.* Routledge. p 2, 75, 77-78.

borders of Lower Egypt and created the Fifteenth Dynasty (also known as the Foreign Dynasty).[21] Salitis and the Kushite kings aligned to consolidate power by subjugating Thebes, surrounding what was left of Egyptian rule to the north with the Hyksos and the south with the Kushite army. The Kerma military flooded Lower Egypt and exacted tribute upon the local rulers, further increasing their financial holdings. One hundred years later, a Theban pharaoh, Ahmose I, rose to power and defeated the Hyksos forces in 1550. Seizing control of Lower Egypt and vanquishing the Hyksos, Egypt soon turned its attention toward the Kushite kingdom to the south.

By 1504 BCE, Pharaoh Thutmose I succeeded in crushing the Kingdom of Kerma, bringing all of Nubia under Egyptian control. Now officially called Kush, Egypt established cities as far south as the Fourth Cataract and established Kush's capital at Napata, making Nubia a client state. During this time (in Egypt referred to as the New Kingdom period, running from circa 1550 to 1075 BCE), the Nubian culture adopted many of Egypt's rituals and customs. Marriages between elite Egyptian and Nubian families were common, and the Egyptian religion, particularly the worship of Amun, became the primary worship of the region.

Archaeological evidence suggests that while Nubia took many of Egypt's social and religious (and therefore burial) customs as their own, the Kingdom of Kush retained many identifying factors, separating it from Egypt. Artwork depicted Kushites with dark skin, close shaved hairstyles, animal skin cloaks, and earrings. The Kushites also retained their highly developed methodology of pottery making, producing some of the most advanced and highly valued ceramics in

---

[21] Ryholt, K. S. B.; Bülow-Jacobsen, Adam. (1997). *The Political Situation in Egypt During the Second Intermediate Period, C. 1800-1550 B.C.* Museum Tusculanum Press. p 131-132.

the world.[22] Egypt and the Kingdom of Kush would coexist peacefully for centuries until a threat arose from elsewhere in Africa.

In circa 748 BCE, forces hailing from Libya began to threaten Egypt from the west. At the request of Egypt, the Kushite king, Piye, assembled his Upper Nubian army and invaded Egypt to assist in repelling the threat. Successfully pushing the invading armies back, Piye then established the Twenty-fifth Dynasty of Egypt, becoming the first outright Nubian pharaoh and establishing his capital at Thebes.

Using their strong governmental experience from Nubia, the Kushite pharaohs of Egypt were known for their stable rule and expansion efforts. Realizing that the Egyptian kingdom was often united through its construction efforts, the son of Piye, Khunefertumre (Taharqa), ordered monuments and temples to be built throughout Lower and Upper Egypt, as well as Kush. He also spared no expense to expand the cities of Memphis and Thebes, and he further established Nubia's Jebel Barkal as a temple and worship center.

After a number of invasion attempts spanning many years, in circa 660 BCE, the Assyrian war machine swept into Thebes and forced the last Nubian pharaoh, Tantamani, from power. Abandoning Thebes, Tantamani retreated to the Nubian city of Meroe and attempted to rule Upper Egypt from Kush. Unable to retake the city from the Assyrians, other Egyptian rivals rose to claim the pharaonic throne.

With Thebes facing invasion from Psamtik I, Tantamani eventually relinquished control of Thebes in 656 BCE and acknowledged Psamtik I as the pharaoh, ending the Nubian dynasties of Egypt.

---

[22] "Pottery in the New Kingdom (about 1550-1069 BC)." (2001). 21 July 2021. https://www.ucl.ac.uk/museums-static/digitalegypt/pottery/nk.html.

Meroe

Most historians classify the final phase of the Upper Nubia's Kushite kingdom as the Meroitic period, named after its capital city of Meroe. Lasting nearly seven hundred years, the Meroitic period ran from approximately 300 BCE to 400 CE.

Much like the city of Kerma thousands of years earlier, Meroe occupied a central location that made it advantageous in controlling trade routes throughout Africa. By using complex irrigation techniques acquired from the Egyptians to the north, the people of Meroe were able to create wide fertile fields and raise an abundance of crops. As a port city on the Nile River, Meroe was strategically positioned to export its goods quickly into the African interior and abroad via the Red Sea.

During the Meroitic period, the most well-known features of ancient Nubia were constructed: the pyramids. Nubian pyramids serves as tombs for the elite of Nubian society—queens, kings, high priests, and local leaders. One necropolis in Meroe contains more pyramids than all of the pyramids of Egypt!

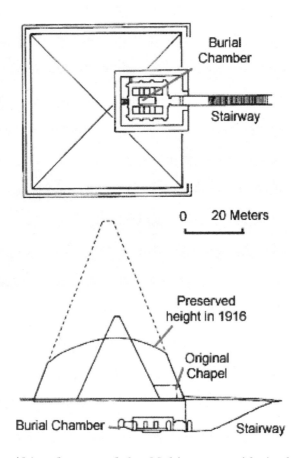

One identifying feature of the Nubian pyramids is that they are substantially narrower at the base and longer at the top, giving Kushite pyramids the appearance of arrow tips jutting from the desert floor. While Egyptian pyramids are two to four times as tall as those of Nubia (the largest Nubian pyramid measures one hundred feet tall, while the Great Pyramid of Giza is four hundred feet tall), Nubian pyramids generally slope at seventy degrees, compared to the typical Egyptian pyramid sloping at fifty degrees.[23] Also, the Nubian pyramids represented tombs but were not the tombs themselves. The burial chambers of Kushite tombs were actually beneath the pyramids. The

---

[23] MacDonald, James. (2015). "The Forgotten Pyramids of Sudan." JSTOR Daily. 21 July 2021. https://daily.jstor.org/forgotten-pyramids-sudan/.

Nubian pyramids served as a monument to the glory of who was buried beneath.

At Meroe, the Kingdom of Kush continued to thrive, even with the ever-present Egyptian empire to the north. Adopting much of the style of Egyptian governance that they had influenced them for over a century, Kush created its own dynastic leadership and versions of religious rituals, especially toward the god Amun. For the first time, Kush began to develop its own written language, even going as far as to create its own alphabet.

Centuries later, with the rise of Rome in Egypt, Kush soon fell into the sightlines of the Mediterranean empire. While famously battling Rome over the centuries, with Kush even penetrating as far as Aswan in 22 BCE, Rome and Kush eventually settled into an uneasy stalemate and established trade.[24]

By 200 CE, the Nobatae people assumed power over the people of Meroe. Originally a nomadic and mercenary warrior culture who sold protection to the kings of Meroe, the Nobatae married into the aristocracy of Kush and assumed control of the empire. As they were highly favored by Rome, the Nobataes' primary role was to use Kush as a buffer between Rome's interests in southern Egypt and rising threats from Ethiopia's Aksum (Axum) and invading tribes from southern Africa. But the power of Aksum rose, and in 350 CE, Ethiopia's King Aksum captured the city of Meroe and destroyed it, causing the area to become abandoned and bringing an end to the Kushite empire.

Christian and Muslim Takeovers and the End of Nubia as an Independent State

While the Nobatae still ruled over the territories of ancient Nubia, their power would never rise to the levels it did during the last days of the Kushite empire. Rome continued to pay Nobatae aristocrats to serve as a buffer zone for Egypt, but alliances between villages and city-states were ever-shifting. In circa 530 CE, the Nobataes united under Silko, naming him king. In 540, King Silko officially converted to Coptic Orthodox Christianity and established Christianity as the sole religion of his kingdom. Now united under a single flag and religion, the Nobatae defeated the Blemmyes and established a capital city at Faras before eventually merging with Makuria and then into the kingdom of Dunqulah (Dongola) in the 6th century.[25, 26]

Like Silko's kingdom a century before it, Dunqulah's primary religion was Christianity. However, in the latter part of the 7th century, Muslim armies from Egypt overran the territory and commanded its leaders to pay tribute to Egypt. For the next seven hundred years, Nubia would remain Christianized before being overtaken by the Mamluk army, who established Nubia's new capital at Alwa.[27]

Arab invasions continued over the next few centuries until the Funj Dynasty of Sennar brought Nubia under its control during the 16th century. The Funj, who were bitter rivals with the Ottoman Empire, fought the encroaching empire to a standstill at Sai Island, establishing a firm border between the territories in 1582. This would be the demarcation line between Egyptian power and Nubian control until the entire area was united by Egypt's Muhammad Ali in 1823, bringing an end to Nubia's independent status. Upon its secession from Egypt in 1956, the area was renamed the Republic of Sudan.

---

[24] Ibid.

[25] Hagg, T. (2002). "Silko's Language: A Retrospect." *A Tribute to Excellence-Studia Aegyptiaca Vol. XVII*. Budapest. p 289-300.

[26] Obluski, Arthur. (1899). "The Rise of Nobadia. Social Changes in Northern Nubia in Late Antiquity." *Journal of Juristic Papyrology* (January 1, 1899). p 28-30.

[27] Augustyn, Adam. (2020). "Nubia." Britannica. 24 July 2021. https://www.britannica.com/place/Nubia.

Chapter 3 – The Prehistoric Cultures of Ancient Nubia

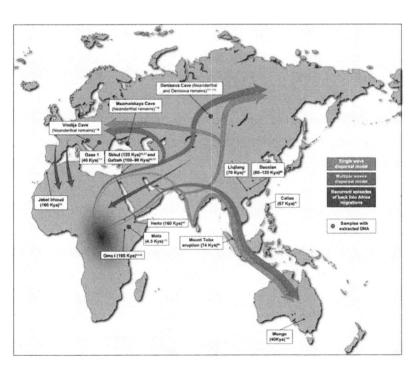

The landscape of prehistoric Nubia was much different than what we see now. While modern southern Egypt and Sudan are now known for their arid desert landscapes, eight thousand years ago, North Africa was covered in windswept grasslands.

Throughout North Africa's existence, the region has moved between wet and dry climates due to the alternating frequency of the North African monsoon. And while the Saharan Desert is currently in a dry cycle (and it is theorized will be until approximately 17,000 CE), its wet cycles brought lush vegetation and life to an area that is presently considered by most to be harsh and brutal.

While evidence exists that shows early hominids were present in North and East Africa 2.4 million years ago, most anthropologists believe that our first human ancestors began venturing into northeast Africa approximately 1 million years ago.[28,29]

Nine thousand years ago, as our early human ancestors adapted to their environments, they began herding animals such as cattle and sheep. Archaeological evidence suggests that this region of Africa was traversed by cattle herders, who moved with their herds throughout the seasons in a nomadic lifestyle. As the regional deserts were then grasslands, ample vegetation was available for animal consumption and migration.

Lower Nubia, then Upper Nubia after it, was host to several mysterious and ancient civilizations whose impact would be felt for millennia. These little-known cultures would have a powerful impact on the history of northeast Africa and would give rise to the eventual Kingdom of Kush, which would rival that of Egypt for centuries.

---

[28] Duval, Mathieu. (2018). "Stone Tools Date Early Humans in North Africa to 2.4 Million Years Ago." The Conversation. 30 June 2021. https://theconversation.com/stone-tools-date-early-humans-in-north-africa-to-2-4-million-years-ago-107617.

[29] Jarus, Owen. (2017). "Ancient Nubia: A Brief History." Live Science. 30 June 2021. https://www.livescience.com/57875-ancient-nubia.html.

- The people of Nabta Playa
- Early Khartoum
- A- and B-Group culture
- C-Group culture
- The Medjay
- Pre-Kerma

The Mysterious Prehistoric Civilization of Nabta Playa

The region known as Nabta Playa is a natural depression located in ancient Nubia (now south Egypt), approximately sixty miles west of Abu Simbel and five hundred miles south of Cairo. In total, Nabta Playa is an area that covers two thousand square miles and is a veritable treasure trove of archaeological remnants of an ancient culture.

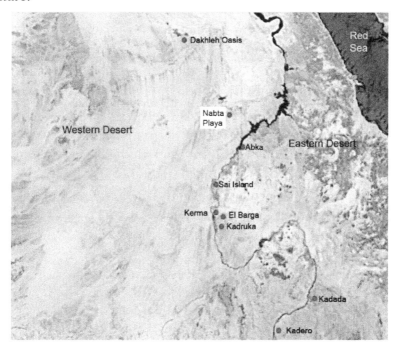

While Nabta Playa is now covered with dry desert sands, it was once filled with temporary lakes (playas) and was the home of an advanced Neolithic civilization dated to approximately 7500 BCE.[30] With the cyclical pattern of the North African monsoon releasing large amounts of water and humidity in the region between 10,000 to 9,000 BCE, Nabta Playa attracted a number of creatures. Evidence suggests that the area of Nabta Playa was highly traversed with giraffes, buffalo, antelope, gazelle, hyenas, and other animals. This naturally attracted humans to the area, who hunted the local animals as prey but who also could rely on the lakes' fresh water for sustenance.

Archaeologist Fred Wendorf, whose excavations date the earliest human settlements of Nabta Playa between 10,000 to 8,000 BCE, believed that the earliest human residents there were pastoralists who herded cattle and possibly sheep. However, this is highly disputed by other researchers who have found that analysis of the cattle bones on-site demonstrated evidence of the animals being roaming cattle. This indicates that the area was not permanently settled but was occupied seasonally by cattle herders looking for abundant water sources. Broken pottery shards and traces of wild sorghum suggest that the region's inhabitants were in touch with other cultures around them (such as those at Khartoum five hundred miles to the south) and thus were nomadic. Study of human skeletal and dental remains located throughout Nabta Playa suggests that the vast majority of its ancient settlers were of African descent from south of the Sahara who moved south to north, whereas those to the north of the Nile's Great Cataract were genetically more similar to Near Eastern and eastern Mediterranean Neolithic populations.[31, 32]

---

[30] Wendorf, Fred; Schild, Romuald. (2013). "Holocene Settlement of the Egyptian Sahara." *The Archeology of Nabta Playa, Volume 1*. p 51-53.

[31] Page, Thomas. (2017). "DNA discovery reveals genetic history of ancient Egyptians." CNN Health. 2 July 2021.
https://edition.cnn.com/2017/06/22/health/ancient-egypt-mummy-dna-genome-heritage/index.html.

Archaeological findings reveal that by the 7th millennium, settlements throughout Nabta Playa became semi-permanent. Evidence of deep wells dot the landscape, and pottery shards reveal trace elements of fruits, sorghum, and various beans, indicating that food storage was a long-term priority of those living in localized sites. The alignment of huts in straight rows throughout various settlements suggests extended contact and organization between communities. And remains of goats and sheep that originated from the areas now known as Saudi Arabia, Iraq, Iran, and Afghanistan are a common discovery, suggesting extensive travel and trade.[33]

By 6000 BCE, evidence reveals that the people of Nabta Playa lived in communities that utilized greater planning, as buildings were being constructed above and below ground using stone for multi-level construction. This was significantly more advanced than the prehistoric homes of the Egyptians to the north upon the Nile River, which share a similar timeline. While it may have been common for nomadic cattle herders to move through the area during the summers (leading to swelling seasonal populations), evidence suggests that several Nabta Playa communities were settled year-round due to the depths of their wells, which were dug deep enough to hold water throughout the year.

What makes Nabta Playa extremely unique, however, is the evidence of organized religion and worship, making Nabta Playa one of the world's first known religious settlements. During his excavations, Wendorf discovered numerous clay-lined chambers with stone roofs, with cattle appearing to be ritually sacrificed and buried inside. Named the "Valley of the Sacrifices," ten burial locations were identified with the remains of cows, goats, and sheep, with cattle appearing to be given a place of honor since they were buried on their

---

[32] Wendorf, Fred; Schild, Romuald. (2013). "Holocene Settlement of the Egyptian Sahara." *The Archeology of Nabta Playa, Volume 1.* p 125-128.

[33] Ness, Immanuel. (2013). *The Global Prehistory of Human Migration.* John Wiley and Sons. p 103.

side with their heads facing west (the west typically being identified with death).[34] This indicates that the early permanent inhabitants of Nabta Playa may have been part of a cattle cult, potentially worshiping cattle deities to influence cattle migration and health, thus increasing the health and prosperity of local communities.

Nabta Playa's Potential Influence upon the Prehistoric Egyptian Faith

Several Egyptologists argue that over the millennia, the Nabta Playa cult may have evolved into the early basis for the Egyptian goddess Hathor, as evidence suggests belief in Hathor traveled south to north along the Nile, with Hathor enjoying greater worship in Upper Egypt and Nubia compared to Lower Egypt of the Nile Delta. Symbolized by the cow, Hathor was highly regarded during Egypt's Predynastic (6000-3150 BCE) and Old Kingdom (2700-2150 BCE) periods, with the goddess linked to the Earth's creation. She was the ruler of the sky, creator of music and dance, and responsible for fertility. Hathor was venerated so much during Egypt's early recorded history that she was considered the Eye of Ra, Ra's feminine aspect responsible for carrying out Ra's vengeance against disorder and chaos.

---

[34] Hill, J (2016). "Nabta Playa Stone Circle." Ancient Egypt Online. 8 July 2021. https://ancientegyptonline.co.uk/nabtaplaya/.

The most stunning discovery at Nabta Playa, however, is that it is home to one of the world's earliest monolithic sites, which potentially could be the oldest archaeoastronomy site in the world. The Nabta Playa megalithic site, the earliest example of a monument presumably organized by religious means in Nubia and Egypt, is believed by many scholars to be the potential birthplace of several Egyptian and Nubian beliefs, including the afterlife. Older than Stonehenge by at least one thousand years, Nabta Playa has invited many guesses as to its purpose since its discovery, causing a great deal of increased controversy over the last forty years.

The Controversy of Nubia's and Egypt's Earliest Monument – The Stone Circle of Nabta Playa (circa 7000–3100 BCE)

Approximately eight thousand to seven thousand years ago, evidence suggests that Nabta Playa was abandoned multiple times during a series of major droughts. This may have led to a need for the local nomadic culture to keep track of seasons, drought cycles, and the alignments of the stars in the sky. Most scholars agree that the mysterious stone monument of Nabta Playa was constructed between 4500 and 3600 BCE to fulfill this purpose; however, a great deal of vocal criticism has challenged this assertion over the last forty years. After an in-depth survey of the site, the UNESCO World Heritage Convention stated the Nabta Playa megalithic monument had "hypothetical solar and stellar alignments" and that a deeper study was recommended.[35]

---

[35] Belmonte, Juan Antonio. (2010). *Heritage Sites of Astronomy and Archaeoastronomy in the context of the UNESCO World Heritage Convention: A Thematic Study.* Paris: International Council on Monuments and Sites/International Astronomical Union. p 119-129.

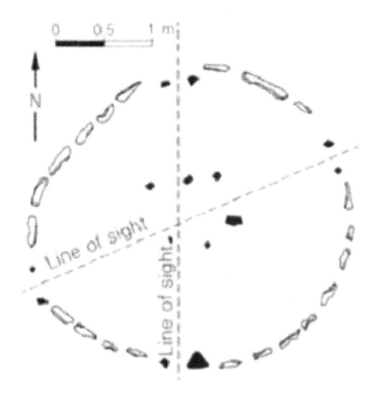

Predating the most well-known stone circle on Earth, Stonehenge, by more than one thousand years, the stone circle of Nabta Playa reveals a great deal of sophistication in its construction. Challenging held assumptions about the ability of prehistoric cultures to organize, quarry, carve, transport, and utilize such large monuments, the largest megaliths at Nabta Playa measure six feet wide by nine feet high and weigh several tons. Global Positioning System (GPS) examination of the megalithic monument reveals that the stones were not placed haphazardly but were aligned to track the summer and winter solstices and the equinoxes and were aligned true north/south, with "gates" marking east to west. The six interior stones, however, do not align to any of the four cardinal directions, which has led to a great deal of conjecture as to their purpose, with some suggesting they marked certain stars in the night sky, which are five alignments that stretch from the central stones to the smaller surrounding stones. These stones are believed to mark the ascension points of the stars Sirius and Dubhe, as well as Mintaka, Alnilam, and Alnitak (the three stars of Orion's Belt). Regardless of the interior stones' purpose, the Nabta Playa megaliths suggest a great deal of organization and planning. To make such a monument happen, a culture that had little recorded knowledge of engineering or complex mathematical concepts would have had to organize a vast number of people to quarry rocks from over one-third of a mile away, move stones that weighed several tons to a central site, and then place the stones in precise spots that marked celestial alignments. This was no simple feat and has led to rather wild theories suggesting that the ancient builders of the Nabta Playa monuments were assisted by extraterrestrial lifeforms. However, careful examination of the monument refutes such far-fetched claims.

Archaeoastronomers, such as astrophysicist Thomas G. Brophy, believe that in drawing lines across the alignment of the stones found at the site, the lines match the direction of the sunrise during the summer solstice on June 21st. Furthermore, archaeoastronomers believe that on that date, the additional lines potentially marked the positions of the constellations Sirius, Dubhe, and the belt of the constellation now known as Orion. Brophy goes on to argue that when taking the precession of the Earth into account, the three stones inside the circle match the stars on what we now call Orion's Belt, and the three other stones represent the shoulder and head stars of Orion and symbolize the movement of the night sky during the Earth's precession. Analyzing the alignments of the larger stones at the site, Brophy believes that they matched with the smaller stones, linking them to the alignment of Orion's Belt in 6400 BCE and 4900 BCE. Evidence revealed through radiocarbon dating of campfires around the circle indicates that the area surrounding the circle was in ritual use during this time, lending circumstantial credence to archaeoastronomers' theories.[36] Brophy would later go on to argue that the Nabta Playa site also held evidence that symbolized the Milky Way Galaxy as it appeared in the sky in 17,500 BCE.[37] If true, being able to track the stars and understanding the "movement" of the stars in the sky over such an extended period indicates that the society of Nabta Playa was extremely advanced with a highly evolved religious function, with theorists such as Graham Hancock going so far as to suggest that Nabta Playa's construction was inspired by alien life.

However, academic research reveals that many of the wilder claims of archaeoastronomers and conspiracy theories fall flat under scrutiny. Recent scholarly articles reveal that many of the early celestial alignment theories were made in error and that claims of extraterrestrial contact were inconsistent with the archaeology present on site. In 2007, an investigative team cast more scholarly doubt on Brophy's claim of the Nabta Playa monument representing the Milky Way Galaxy in 17,500 BCE, going on record to state, "These extremely early dates as well as the proposition that the nomads had

---

[36] Brophy, Thomas; Rosen, P (2005) *Satellite Imagery Measures of the Astronomically Aligned Megaliths at Nabta Playa.* Mediterranean Archaeology and Archaeometry, Number 5. p 15-24.

[37] Brophy, Thomas. (2002). *The Origin Map: Discovery of a Prehistoric, Megalithic, Astrophysical Map and Sculpture of the Universe.* iUniverse, Illustrated Edition.

contact with extraterrestrial life are inconsistent with the archaeological record. Inference in archaeoastronomy must always be guided and informed by archaeology, especially when substantial field work has been performed in the region."[38]

Instead of far-fetched theories suggesting contact with alien life, the monument of Nabta Playa, while still an engineering marvel for a prehistoric culture, was designed for simpler purposes: to keep track of seasonal and star alignments for survival, animal herding and movement, and water cycles (rainy seasons, etc.).

---

[38] Cott, J. (1998). "Oldest Astronomical Megalith Alignment Discovered in Southern Egypt by Science Team." University of Colorado – Boulder.

Evidence demonstrates that the area surrounding the Nabta Playa monument was in use as early as 6100 to 5600 BCE and was used as a religious center, where it was believed the surrounding tribes and nomads would gather in large ceremonial groups on the surrounding dunes. Radiocarbon-dated fire remnants and cattle bones that have been unearthed surrounding the megalithic monument suggest that these ceremonies featured animal sacrifices, where cattle were potentially offered up to the gods, possibly to influence rain or solar cycles. These bones are believed to predate the monument by one thousand years. By 5400 BCE, a new group entered the region, most likely nomadic settlers from the south. These mysterious inhabitants introduced the practice of burying their sacrificed cattle in large burial mounds, which were covered stone structures smoothed over with clay.

Six hundred years later, in 4800 BCE, the first stones began to mark the site, loosely aligned with the summer solstice. These stones marked the three weeks leading up to the solstice and the three weeks after, which also importantly marked the beginning of the rainy season. Evidence suggests that the larger stones were moved into place over a thousand-year period, between 4500 and 3600 BCE. While the exact purpose of the larger megaliths is not known, it is theorized that the area evolved to become a necropolis that utilized astronomical observations, potentially indicating the beginnings of a formalized belief in the afterlife, as all sacrificial remains, human remains, and rock carvings dated to this time indicate the importance of being pointed north.[39]

---

[39] Malville, J McKim; Schild, R.; Wendorf, F.; Brenmer, R. (2007). "Astronomy of Nabta Playa." *African Skies/Cieux Africains. Vol 11.* p 2. https://ui.adsabs.harvard.edu/abs/2007AfrSk..11....2M/abstract,

Early Khartoum (circa 5000 BCE)

At present-day Khartoum, the capital of Sudan, the White Nile and the Blue Nile
interse

It was at this site, over seven thousand years ago, that a culture referred to as the Khartoum Mesolithic thrived. In 1944, British archaeologist A. J. Arkell began excavating and dating a site discovered by a nearby hospital. Arkell referred to this site as evidence of a culture he dubbed as "Early Khartoum." While the dig revealed no examples of houses or living areas, the archaeologist was able to determine that the remains that were discovered indicated continual habitation. Arkell surmised that the culture lived along the hospitable sandy banks of the Blue Nile and that the culture's people existed by "hunting, fishing and gathering wild fruits and river snails."[40]

---

[40] Arkell, A. J. (1945). "The Excavation of An Ancient Site at Khartoum." *Sudan Notes and Records, Volume 26, No. 2.* p 329-331.

One of the most interesting finds from the site was the discovery of pottery shards, indicating that the Khartoum Mesolithic people created arguably some of the world's most ancient pottery. While no pottery vessels were found whole, these pottery "bowls with simple rims" were decorated with what Arkell referred to as "wavy line wares." These wavy lines were imprinted onto the pottery clay as it was drying, most likely by using the spines of locally caught catfish, as a great number of bones were scattered throughout the dig site. This decorated pottery further demonstrated advanced skills such as using primitive kilns or trench fires to create enduring pieces, skills that would not become commonplace until three thousand years later during the Naqada period of Egypt.

As no evidence was uncovered of domesticated animals at the Early Khartoum site nor of sustained agriculture, it is believed sustenance for the culture was provided by hunting, fishing, and gathering. Over 270 fragmented and whole harpoons and spearheads were uncovered at the site. A number of these heads were decorated with the same carved lines that decorated localized pottery shards. Smaller pieces are believed to be evidence of arrow usage, indicating that the Khartoum Mesolithic people had extensive knowledge of complex and organized hunting practices. Evidence also exists that the Khartoum Mesolithic people consumed wild grain. Arkell's excavation uncovered several crescent instruments that were made from quartz rock. It is believed these instruments were used to grind wild grain into flour. No evidence exists, however, of extended farming practices.[41]

---

[41] "Nubia: Early Khartoum." (2002). University College London. 1 July 2021. https://www.ucl.ac.uk/museums-static/digitalegypt/nubia/earlykhart.html.

The Rise and Fall of the A- and B-Group Cultures in Prehistoric Nubia (3800-3100 BCE)

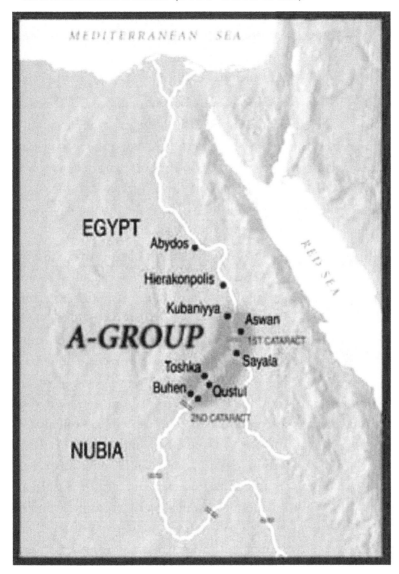

A new civilization rose between the First and Second Cataracts of the Nile River beginning in 3800 BCE. Believed to be the first Nubian culture with powerful rulers, archaeologists have discovered remnants of this prehistoric civilization from Kubaniyya in the north to Buhen in the south.

While few details are known about this ancient Nubian culture, it is known that this civilization traded extensively with that of prehistoric Egypt and utilized complex burial customs, suggesting an evolving belief in the afterlife and religious ceremonies.[42]

Referred to simply as the A- and B-Group cultures, this civilization mined iron-oxide gemstones in the Libyan Desert to the west and gold from the Eastern Desert of the Sahara. This culture's power base on the Nile also gave them access to ebony, ivory, and incense. In turn, these items were traded with the kingdoms of Egypt to the north for olive oil and other goods from the Mediterranean, enabling A-Group culture rulers to consolidate their power and wealth.

The first artifacts of the A- and B-Group cultures were discovered in 1907 by Egyptologist George Reisner. While originally classified as two potentially separate cultures, Harry Sidney Smith refuted the A- and B-Group theory in 1966 by proving that the people of the B-Group culture were simply the remains of an impoverished subset of the A-Group culture.[43] Most of what is now known of the A-Group culture comes from the examination of their cemeteries, as the A-Group culture apparently took great care in honoring their dead by constructing large necropolises to entomb their remains. The discovered remains of over three thousand graves have been attributed to the A-Group culture, and tombs typically contained remnants of pottery, ceramics, and other items of value in life and of potential value in the afterlife. Adults were typically wrapped in leather and positioned north to south on mats made of reed, and A-Group necropolises contained approximately fifty oval pits for

---

[42] "Ancient Nubia: A-Group 3800 – 3100 BC." Oriental Institute, University of Chicago. 10 July 2021. https://oi.uchicago.edu/museum-exhibits/nubia/ancient-nubia-group-3800%E2%80%933100-bc.

[43] Smith, Harry Sidney. "The Nubian B-Group." *Kush: Journal of the Sudan Antiquities Service.* Vol 14. p 69-124.

singular burials or pits containing funerary niches for multiple bodies. Genetically, the bodies found in A-Group tombs typically compare to those found in Upper Nubia's later Kerma culture, although they also share traits with Ethiopians and those of later Meroitic cultures. On average, women were approximately five feet one inch tall, and men were five feet eight inches, and remnants of well-preserved hair indicate that hair was straight and of darker color.[44]

Like the Nubian cultures dated before it, a distinctive feature of the A-Group culture was its pottery. A-Group pottery was highly advanced for its time, and several examples have been fully recovered from excavation sites throughout Sudan and Egypt. Formed in the shape of bowls and baskets, A-Group pottery was detailed with puncture and wave designs, and they were often painted, then smoothed out before being fired mouth downward. This made the interior of the pots darken with heat and ash while leaving the outsides smooth and decorative.[45]

---

[44] Shinnie, Peter L. (1996). *Ancient Nubia*. Routledge, Taylor & Francis. p 50.

[45] "Ancient Nubia: A-Group Pottery." Oriental Institute, University of Chicago. 19 July 2021. https://oi.uchicago.edu/museum-exhibits/nubia/ancient-nubia-group-pottery.

Archaeologists theorize that while the A-Group culture was considered powerful for its time, much of its culture was influenced by their Egyptian neighbors to the north, whereas it appears little of Egyptian culture was influenced by the A-Group culture other than the importation of gold and gemstones.

One major indicator of this theory was the discovery of an incense censer in an A-Group cemetery in Qustul dated between 3200 and 3100 BCE. Believing that the censer bears carvings indicating rulership, the incense burner has drawn comparison to those discovered in the Abydos region of Egypt. However, similar Egyptian censers are dated four hundred years earlier, suggesting that the rulers of A-Group cultures took on symbols of authority from their neighbors to the north.[46] Also, while many of the A-Group's tombs bear similar styled markings and items of ancient Egypt's Naqada people, very little of A-Group's cultural trade goods made their way into Naqada's tombs. While the cultures comparatively existed and did trade with one another, Egyptologist Kathryn Bard states,

---

[46] Torok, Laszlo. *Between Two Worlds: The Frontier Region Between Ancient Nubia and Egypt, 3700 BC – AD 500*. In Probleme Der Agyptologie. Leiden, Brill.

"Naqada cultural burials contain very few Nubian craft goods, which suggests that while Egyptian goods were exported to Nubia and were buried in A-Group graves, A-Group goods were of little interest further north."[47]

Additionally, A-Group nobility seal impressions have been discovered that depict the pictographic symbology of their northern Egyptian neighbors, particularly that of the kings of the Naqada II and III phases. While the language of the A-Group culture is not known (and highly debated among scholars), the seals of A-Group leaders often depicted a bow above a rectangle. This may have been one of ancient Egypt's first references to Nubia as the Land of the Bow— Ta-Seti. The descendants of the A-Group culture's bowmen would eventually become prized commodities as mercenaries in the Egyptian armies and would gain fame as warriors in the Persian military thousands of years later.[48]

---

[47] Bard, Kathryn A. (2015). *An Introduction to the Archaeology of Ancient Egypt*. Wiley Publishers. p 110.

[48] "Ancient Nubia: A-Group 3800 – 3100 BC." Oriental Institute, University of Chicago. 10 July 2021. https://oi.uchicago.edu/museum-exhibits/nubia/ancient-nubia-group-3800%E2%80%933100-bc.

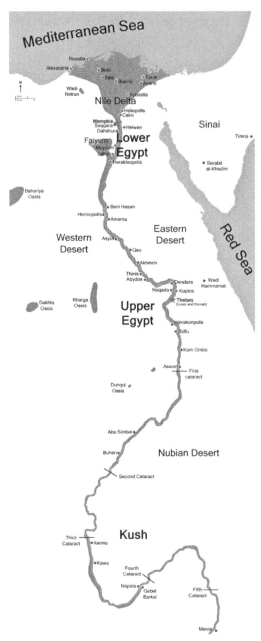

Evidence suggests that Nubia's A-Group culture diminished at the time of Egypt's First Dynasty (3100–2900 BCE) with the rise of King Narmer. Narmer was the first king of Egypt who united the towns and villages along the northern Nile, bringing together Lower and Upper

Egypt for the first time in history. Narmer established Memphis as his capital, but he crafted his necropolis in Abydos in the south, increasing Egypt's military presence along its southern border. As the power of Egypt grew, the nation began to flex its military might along its southern border and began to create incursions and raids to claim the resources of its weaker Nubian neighbor. Over the next five hundred years, Egypt would continue to strip Lower Nubia of its mineral wealth and erase the A-Group culture from existence.

During the reign of the Fourth Dynasty pharaoh, Snefru (ruled circa 2613-2589), Egypt's military expeditions advanced as far as the Great Cataract (Second Cataract) and established an outpost at Buhen, making Buhen the earliest Egyptian settlement in ancient Nubia. At Buhen, the Egyptians built one of the world's first copper factories and constructed quarries to mine granite and gneiss for transport back to Egypt.[49,50]

During Egypt's Sixth Dynasty, Egypt began to establish firmer trade connections with the ancient Nubian tribes. During the reign of King Merenre, the third king of Egypt's Sixth Dynasty, the king named Harkhuf as the governor of Upper Egypt. Harkhuf, in turn, would serve as governor for twenty years (2290-2270 BCE).

Extensive records exist of Harkhuf's travels and exploits throughout ancient Nubia. At one point in his travels, Harkhuf even counseled Nubian tribes to cease warfare with Libyan tribes in order to keep Egypt's trade routes open. For his efforts, the Nubian tribes gifted the governor with over three hundred pack donkeys and an armed escort to transport ebony, ivory, and incense back to Elephantine. But while Harkhuf was honored among many chieftains of the Nubian tribes, his trade efforts began unifying the tribes of the

---

[49] Gayar, El Sayed; Jones MP. (1989). "A Possible Source of Copper Ore Fragments Found at the Old Kingdom Town of Buhen." *The Journal of Egyptian Archaeology, Vol 75.* p 31-40.

[50] Augustyn, Adam ED. "Nubia." Britannica. 13 July 2021. https://www.britannica.com/place/Nubia.

Nubian lands, which would eventually challenge Egypt's hold on the region.[51, 52, 53]

---

[51] "Ancient Nubia: A-Group 3800 – 3100 BC." Oriental Institute, University of Chicago. 10 July 2021. https://oi.uchicago.edu/museum-exhibits/nubia/ancient-nubia-group-3800%E2%80%933100-bc.

[52] Augustyn, Adam ED. "Nubia." Britannica. 13 July 2021. https://www.britannica.com/place/Nubia.

[53] "Harkhuf, governor of Aswan." Britannica. 13 July 2021. https://www.britannica.com/biography/Harkhuf.

C-Group Culture (circa 2400-1550 BCE)

While there is no firm agreement on where ancient Nubia's C-Group culture originally came from, what is known is that they existed near the end of Egypt's Old Kingdom and that the Egyptians classified C-Group settlements into small states or tribes. Three of these states were called Irjet, Wawat, and Setju.[54]

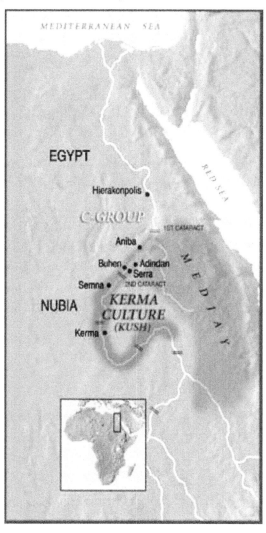

---

[54] Wilkinson, Toby. (2013). *The Egyptian World*. Routledge, Taylor and Francis. p 405.

Historians believe that the C-Group culture was an amalgamation of tribal remnants of the earlier A-Group culture and nomadic migrants, who brought the customs of their sub-Saharan cattle cultures into Lower Nubia. Due to leaving no written evidence about themselves nor a centralized location, George Reisner, who was the first to excavate A-Group culture evidence in modern times, named this more recent culture the C-Group.[55]

At the time of the C-Group's existence, the area of Lower Nubia between El-Kubanieh (near Aswan) and modern-day Eritrea was much more favorable for sustaining life than today. Dental and DNA evidence bears out that the people of the C-Group were a mix of farmers and nomadic herders who moved with their cattle during the seasons.

C-Group homes had stone foundations with small central pits used for fires and open roofs, presumably for cooking food and for heating during cold nights. Recovered pottery shows, like their A-Group ancestors, complex ceramic constructions and designs but also an evolving mastery of artistic representation. One of the more popular motifs depicted on their ceramics was that of cattle, further indicating the daily and religious importance of cattle in the C-Group culture.[56]

---

[55] Bianchi, Robert. (2004). *Daily Life of the Nubians*. Greenwood Publishing Group. p 33.

[56] "Nubia Gallery: The Chicago Cattle Bowl." Oriental Institute, University of Chicago. 19 July 2021. https://oi.uchicago.edu/museum-exhibits/nubia/chicago-cattle-bowl.

Like the A-Group culture before it, most of what historians know about the C-Group culture comes from their tombs. C-Group tombs were placed inside simple stone circles, and the bodies were buried in small pits at the circle's center. Some of the C-Group's later tombs featured an additional pit added to the east side of the larger one, and evidence reveals that these pits were for offerings (it is not known, however, whether these offerings were for the dead or the gods). Larger tombs were more detailed, with the primary burial chamber lined with local stones and rocks, and it is believed that these tombs were created for localized figures of importance. Like the A-Group culture before it, graves typically contained items that may have been important to the deceased in life or were needed after death.[57] This indicates that the people of the C-Group culture believed in an afterlife and had developed advanced religious customs.

While the C-Group was generally thought to have been made up of farmers and herders, near the end of the C-Group's existence, this perception changes. The earliest C-Group graves featured few

---

[57] Wharton, William. (1960). *The Sudan in Pre-History and History: A Handbook for Students.* Saint Joseph's Press. p 24.

weapons in the tombs. However, near the end of the C-Group culture's existence, many of its tombs contained daggers, swords, and war axes. Additionally, as the C-Group culture actively traded extensively with southern Egypt, Egyptian goods began to find their way into C-Group tombs, including amulets, hand-crafted gold necklaces, and ceramics.

During Egypt's First Intermediate Period (circa 2100 BCE), the Egyptians referred to the C-Group people of Lower Nubia as the Nehasyu. Trade activity between Egypt and the Nehasyu was very strong, and Aswan was the primary importation point for all of Egypt's goods that were pulled from southern and eastern Africa. Through Nubia, Egypt imported the exotic animals used in their religious temples, the ivory and ebony prized in their jewelry, the copper and gold used in their décor and treasuries, and the granite used in their building projects.

While Egypt generally controlled the lands of Lower Nubia, thus the C-Group people, evidence suggests that Egypt and Nubia coexisted peacefully. DNA and dental evidence demonstrate the existence of mixed marriages and children. Nubians who married into Egyptian families were buried in the complex Egyptian style instead of their simple circle tombs. It is widely accepted that several pharaohs, such as Mentuhotep II (who became the first pharaoh of Egypt's Middle Kingdom period and reigned from 2060 to 2009 BCE) and Amenemhet I (the first ruler of the Twelfth Dynasty, ruling from 1939 to 1910 BCE) were descended from Nubian ancestry. However, though several pharaohs may have genetically had Nubian ancestry, for all intents and purposes, these pharaohs were culturally Egyptian through and through. Scholar F. J. Yurco wrote, "Egyptian rulers of Nubian ancestry had become Egyptians culturally; as pharaohs, they exhibited typical Egyptian attitudes and adopted typical Egyptian policies."[58]

Throughout the C-Group's existence, Nubian archers and soldiers were hired by Egyptian governors to bolster their armies, and C-Group-styled cemeteries even appear in southern Egypt, particularly at Upper Egypt's capital city of Nekhen. Firm evidence also exists of C-Group settlements being built around Egyptian outposts and forts, indicating their importance to the Egyptian military.[59] Nubian bowmen who served in the Egyptian military appear to have been culturally welcomed into Egypt, particularly in the Egyptian town of Gebelein, now known as Naga el-Gherira.

As the power of Egypt grew during its Middle Kingdom period (2030–1650 BCE), Egypt eventually assumed control of the lands of the C-Group culture, further stripping Lower Nubia of its resources as it did with the A-Group before it. As the region became sparse and as

---

[58] Yurco, F. J. (1989). "Were The Ancient Egyptians Black or White?" *Biblical Archaeology Review.* Vol 15, no 5.

[59] Torok, Laszlo. *Between Two Worlds: The Frontier Region Between Ancient Nubia and Egypt, 3700 BC – AD 500.* In Probleme Der Agyptologie. Leiden, Brill.

Egypt turned its attention inward, Lower Nubia was soon claimed by Kerma to the south. The archaeological record of the C-Group culture ceased with the conquest of Nubia during the Eighteenth Dynasty of Egypt when the Nubian lands were overrun by Thutmose I in 1500 BCE.

The Medjay (1800-1500 BCE)

Coexisting with the C-Group culture was that of the Medjay. While similar to the C-Group, the Medjay confined themselves primarily to the Eastern Desert region near the Second Cataract and were nomadic. Also called the Pan-Grave culture, the Medjay began to settle the Nubian region circa 1800 BCE and were believed to come from near the Red Sea.[60]

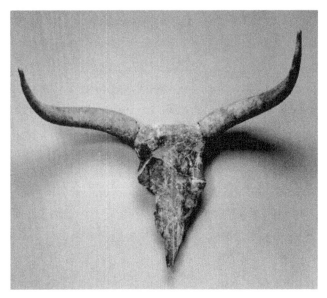

The distinctive feature of the Medjay was a shallow grave with a sloped bottom. The graves were often encircled with the painted skulls of horned animals, or the skulls were buried next to the bodies

---

[60] Naser, Claudia. (2012). "Nomads at the Nile: Towards an Archaeology of Interaction." *The History of the Peoples of the Eastern Desert.* UCLA Cotsen Institute of Archaeology Press. p 81-89.

of the deceased. The graves of the Medjay were typically sparse with few bits of jewelry (such as necklaces), shells, and pottery.

However, unlike their C-Group counterparts, who appeared to be fairly peaceful in their early history, Medjay pan-graves were packed with an abundance of weapons, as the Medjay were often hired by the Egyptian military to operate as scouts and advance infantry, especially during Egypt's conflicts with the Hyksos and Kush.

Like the A and C Group cultures, the Medjay did not leave behind written records. However, due to their apparent bravery and fearlessness in battle, the title Medjay in Egyptian culture later came to refer to a group of elite warriors who defended areas of high security, royal palaces, tombs, and border control.

Pre-Kerma & Early Kerma Cultures

While much of ancient Nubia's known prehistoric culture is confined to Lower Nubia (northern Nubia), the seeds of an advanced civilization to the south in the Upper Nubian region were beginning to sprout as well.

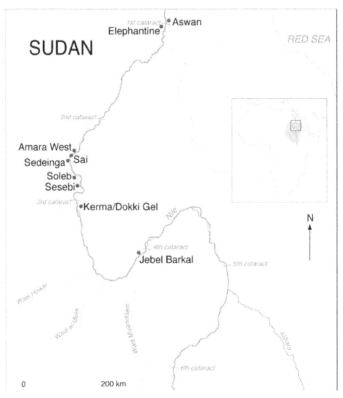

Evidence exists that the northern A-Group culture of Lower Nubia began to trickle south of the Nile's Third Cataract between 3500 and 3000 BCE and settled in what was then a stretch of abundant grasslands, beginning to intermix with a somewhat indigenous culture. The soil in this area could support the growth of several types of crops, and broken A-Group pottery shards found in the region bear remnants of seeds. As the A-Group culture began to create permanent settlements in the region, the various local cultures synthesized with one another and became a group that is classified as the Pre-Kerma culture.

Pre-Kerma culture evolved between 3200 and 2600 BCE, with the people settling between Sai Island, located midway between the Great and Third Cataracts, and an area called Kerma, slightly to the south of the Third Cataract. A virtual archaeological treasure trove, the settlements of the Pre-Kerma people have yielded storage pits filled with the similarly styled red and black topped pottery of the A-Group culture to the north, which were packed with cereals and local seeds. As the local Pre-Kerma civilization enjoyed extensive agriculture and favorable environmental conditions, it enabled the villages to grow to much larger sizes than their neighbors to the north. And since the Pre-Kerma culture was far enough away from Egypt, it was allowed to thrive in relative isolation from the powerful northern empire.

Circa 3200 BCE, the village of Kerma began to blossom into a regional power. By 2600 BCE, Kerma entered the Middle Kerma period, and its primary city was made up of a collection of fifty circular huts, each measuring approximately twelve feet to twenty-one feet. Three large rectangular buildings were believed to serve administrative and religious functions, and they lay at the center of the complex. Within the site, archaeologists have discovered areas for animal husbandry, as well as over five hundred storage areas for cereals and grains. Surrounded by fortifications and watchtowers, the interior of the 2600 BCE Kerma complex measured approximately twenty-four acres. This indicates a complex societal structure where surrounding people groups could retreat into the fortified structure when threatened by outside sources and also store valuables and goods essential for the people group's survival.[61]

---

[61] Honegger, M. (2018). "The Kingdoms of Nubia, From Kerma to Meroe." Paris, p. 59-81.

During the Middle Kerma period, Kerma traded and intermingled with the C-Group culture to the north, as it had done with the A-Group culture. However, unlike the earlier Pre-Kerma culture, the Middle Kerma culture distinctly held onto its own culture and societal functions and began to dominate its neighbors in Middle Nubia.

The southern governor of Egypt, Harkhuf, in approximately 2280 BCE, wrote that the Lower Nubian tribes of Setju, Wawat, and Irjet were united under a powerful ruler, prompting him to travel south to seek trade agreements with Egypt and the kingdoms of Upper Nubia. By 2000 BCE, all archaeological evidence of the C-Group culture vanishes from the record in Upper Nubia, indicating Kerma's growing power throughout the region.

By 1750 BCE, the city of Kerma had grown exponentially, as it was home to over ten thousand people, and its king began to rule Upper Nubia as an empire—an empire that would soon rise to challenge the Egyptian kingdom's dominion over northeastern Africa.[62]

---

[62] "The Story of Africa." www.bbc.co.uk. BBC World Service.

Chapter 4 – The Rise and Fall of the Middle and Classic Kerma Cultures

Cultures do not exist in vacuums. The true timelines of kingdoms and empires do not rise in straight unimpeded lines and then immediately fall precariously. Rather, cultures and their timelines dance and move in rhythm with the environmental factors around them, rising and falling, then falling and rising with elements that are often beyond their control.

Since the Kerma culture did not leave us a written language, the majority of what we know of Kerma's history and society comes to us from the Egyptian and archaeological records. However, modern archaeology has shed great light on the Kerma culture, slowly revealing secrets that have been hidden for thousands of years.

Much of Kerma's history is inextricably tied to that of ancient Egypt. But the reader will find that at a crucial moment during Kerma's slow rise to power in Upper Nubia, the neighboring Egyptian empire, which occupied Lower Nubia, began to face its greatest challenge, providing the rulers of Kerma with an opportunity that they could not refuse.

Middle and Early-Classic Kerma, Center of the Early Kushite Kingdom

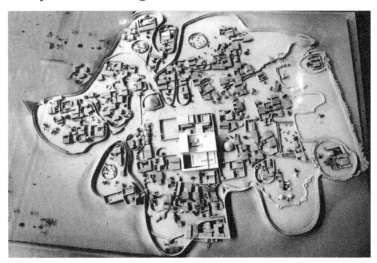

Due to using Lower Nubia as a buffer between it and the Egyptian empire, the city of Kerma thrived along the Nile River and soon found itself the most powerful city-state of ancient Nubia. During its Middle Kerma phase (circa 2050–1750 BCE), Kerma influenced the lives of all who lived between Sai Island (located between the Great and Third Cataracts) and the Fourth Cataract, offering Kerma an expansive kingdom. It was during this period that Egyptian rulers began to refer to Upper Nubia as the Kingdom of Kush, while Nubians referred to the city of Kerma as *Doki*, meaning "Red Hill."

Like Egypt, Middle and Classic Kerma were governed by a ruling class whose status was dependent upon lineage. Evidence suggests that the priest class was determined in the same manner, and kings and priests governed the society in tandem. Due to its location south of the Third Cataract, Kerma was able to control the flow of goods from central Africa south to north *and* controlled the western to eastern flow. This gave Kerma the ability to control trade from lower Africa to the Mediterranean, enabling them to exact taxes and tolls throughout the continent to the Near East. Administrators developed business practices and watched over trade, livestock, hunting, and fishing. As

Kerma was outside of Egypt's boundaries and reach, it quickly rose to dominate trade and began raking in massive wealth.

While Kerma is best remembered as a metropolitan city that dominated local trade, the Kerma culture was primarily rural. By developing complex agricultural practices, the people of the Kerma culture were able to provide its growing population with necessary foods, such as grains, peas, lentils, dates, and melons. Domesticated cattle, sheep, and goats were highly prized and were often used as status indicators within the cities and outside of them. Opportunities also existed in the mines and quarries, where gold, copper, and carnelian were in abundance.

Similar to their Lower Nubian neighbors, Kerma was known for its fierce warriors and archers. However, unlike their tribal neighbors to the north, Kerma developed a highly trained and unified military, and in many regards, it resembled a militarized society. Called Ta-Seti ("Land of the Bow"), the elite of Kerma's military were highly prized and were often hired to train the soldiers of militaries throughout Africa and the Mediterranean. Every single soldier within Kerma's army was trained to use the bow, and evidence suggests that soldiers crafted their own bows to their specifications.

The Kerma bow was unique. Unlike the short bow employed by neighboring kingdoms, the Kerma bow was approximately six feet tall. By using palm fiber as string, the Kerma bow was capable of firing arrows over longer distances than other bows at the time, and its extremely powerful shorter shots were capable of punching through most known types of armor. Kerma arrows were fletched with eagle and goose feathers and utilized metal tips, indicating the use of complex metallurgy. Arrows buried with deceased Kermite soldiers often bore the remnants of poison, suggesting archers would dip their arrow tips in poison before launching them at their enemies.[63]

---

[63] Caryl, Sue. (2018). "The Kingdoms of Kush." National Geographic. 20-7-21. https://www.nationalgeographic.org/media/kingdoms-kush/.

The armies of Kerma were also proficient with spears and also adapted the terrifying khepesh sword into their arsenal after the importation of Egyptian swords in 2000 BCE. The khepesh sword was a frightening weapon in the hands of a Kerma soldier. Khepesh swords were typically twenty-four inches in length and were curved on the inside, designed to hook the enemy's shield or arm. The outside curve of the blade was polished and honed razor-sharp, and it was designed for hacking and slashing. Initially made of bronze, khepesh swords evolved from the crescent-shaped battle-ax and came to be used in their place, as the khepesh was far more efficient and lethal to use in battle.[64] Kerma soldiers were trained to use the khepesh alongside shields, but in the absence of shields, they were trained to use their sword in tandem with knives, using the sword to hook shields out of the way to deliver stabbing blows with the smaller weapon.

---

[64] Hamblin, William. (2006). *Warfare in the Ancient Near East*. Routledge. p 66 – 71.

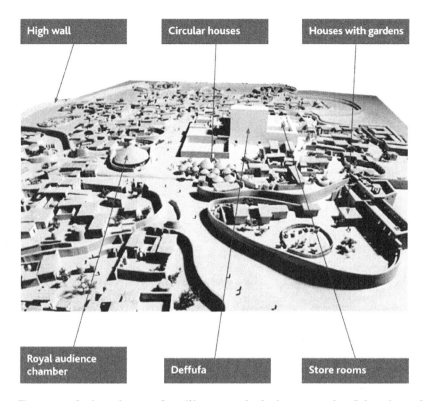

Due to their advanced military and their control of local trade routes, the cities of Kerma were incredibly advanced, featuring workshops that produced jewelry, ceramics, metal goods, and weapons. Kerma itself was said to have over ten thousand people and was surrounded by large walls, which protected residential areas that were connected by planned roads to markets, necropolises, areas set aside for religious functions, and its massive palace.

One of the most well-known and dominant archaeological features of the Kerma culture was the deffufa. The remains of three deffufas exist today, hinting at the grandeur of the Kerma kingdom. Made of mudbrick (deffufa, in Arabic, is defined as great mass or pile*)*, the deffufa was a ceremonial temple that rose high into the air. Archaeologists believe that the tops of the mudbrick monuments were reserved for the religious functions of the priestly elite, who worshiped versions of the same gods as their Egyptian neighbors. The tall mudbrick construction of the deffufas enabled their interiors to remain cool, providing year-round protection from the intense heat of the mid-afternoon sun. The columned interiors allowed for air to flow freely throughout the interior, indicating advanced engineering and planning. The interior walls of the deffufas were usually tiled and painted, and the walls of the Western Deffufa in Kerma were lined with gold.[65]

Of the remaining three deffufas in existence, the most impressive is the Western Deffufa, which lay within the walls of Kerma. The base of the Western Deffufa ran 82 feet by 164 feet and rose over 60 feet into the air. Made up of at least three stories, the Western Deffufa dominated the skyline of the city of Kerma, drawing the eye of all who ventured within a mile of the city. An interior wall surrounded the deffufa on all sides, serving as a boundary that separated it from the populace of the city. The interior of the deffufa was reserved for religious functions and the work of the priest class.

---

[65] Caryl, Sue. (2018). "The Kingdoms of Kush." National Geographic. 20-7-21. https://www.nationalgeographic.org/media/kingdoms-kush/.

A mile east of the Western Deffufa are the remains of the Eastern Deffufa, measuring a bit shorter than its contemporary at two stories high. Surrounded by over thirty thousand white and black pebble-covered graves, researchers believe the Eastern Deffufa to have held a funerary function. The interior walls still depict local wildlife using red, yellow, azure, and sable, while two long halls with column supports run throughout the interior.[66, 67]

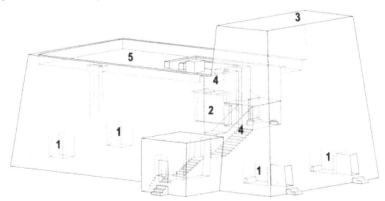

The graves and tombs that surround the Eastern Deffufa demonstrate complex burial customs, indicating a defined view of the afterlife. Unearthed graves from the Middle and early Classic Kerma periods, such as the tomb of who is believed to have been one of the great Kerma kings, demonstrate elaborate burial planning and building, as well as human and animal sacrifice. At the necropolis surrounding the Eastern Deffufa, four large graves still remain, which lie in rows encircled with smaller circular mound graves. Altogether, the diameter of the four large graves and smaller graves measure thirty feet, while the larger mounds are covered with enough white and black stones and pebbles to measure ten feet high.

---

[66] Bietak, Manfred. (2014). *The C-Group Culture and the Pan Grave Culture*. Austrian Archaeological Institute.

[67] Clammer, Paul. (2005). *Bradt Travel Guide Sudan*. Bradt Travel Guides. p 159 – 160.

The interior of the mounds reveals an elaborate tomb complex lined with mudbrick walls that were once presumably painted and decorated in a similar style to the Eastern Deffufa. A path runs along the diameter and eventually terminates at a wooden vault door. Inside the door, at the center of the complex, was the (presumed) king's vaulted chamber. A carved stone bed was found inside the vault, and it is believed that over one thousand cattle and three hundred human lives were sacrificed to honor the passing of the individual within to assist him in the afterlife.[68]

As Kerma moved from its Middle phase to its Classic phase, its territory began to spread into Egypt's holdings in Lower Nubia. And by 1750 BCE, Kerma would arguably rival Egypt in both size and military might.

The Egyptian Element and the Twist of Fate

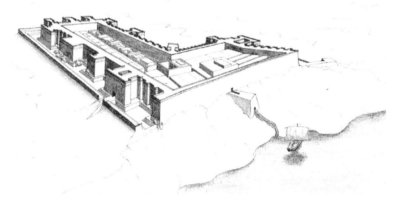

By 2000 BCE, Egypt had dominated northeastern Africa for over a thousand years. Its ever-expanding empire, religious might, and powerful gods were fixtures of everyday life for not just the people within the empire but also those who surrounded it. The Egyptian civilization was the machine that drove goods and services along the

---

[68] Education Development Center. (2015). "Kerma, the First Nubian City." Nubianet. https://web.archive.org/web/20151106023332/http://www.nubianet.org/home/index.html.

Nile River. Its trade contracts with villages and tribes along the Nile throughout Nubia afforded the elite members of Lower and Upper Nubian societies opportunities for great riches. In turn, this enabled the cultures along the Nile to grow wealthy, expanding their villages and kingdoms. The Egyptian military machine provided Nubian mercenaries with continual work, funneling money and security to their families back home. And while Egypt created outposts and fortifications along the borders of their empire, there are few records of major conflicts with the immediate surrounding cultures, even though small skirmishes were common.

Referred to as the Kingdom of Kush by Pharaoh Mentuhotep II (r. 2060–2009 BCE), Egypt saw great risk from the large kingdom to the south. After building a fortress at Abu, the pharaoh used this fortification to launch assaults across Lower Nubia but was unable to penetrate past the Great Cataract. This left Kerma's culture and its power base free to expand along the lower Nile, far enough away from the direct threat of the Egyptian military, as Lower Nubia offered a natural buffer to Egypt's encroaching empire.

Lower Nubia, however, was not so lucky. Circa 1872 BCE, the prized location of Wawat, with its easy access to gold, timber, and ivory, had successfully been seized and was ruled for over one hundred years by local Lower Nubian tribes. Referred to as the "miserable Nubians," the pharaohs of Egypt's Eleventh Dynasty desired to seize Wawat from Nubian control but were constantly rebuffed in their efforts. In 1971 BCE, Senusret I, the second pharaoh of the Twelfth Dynasty, assumed the Egyptian throne and served as co-regent with his father, Amenemhat I. Senusret I desired to continue his father's expansion efforts, with the goal of permanently extending Egypt's southern border into Nubia. Bolstering their military forces along the southern border by hiring mercenaries and scouts from the Nubian territories, Senusret I ordered an expedition farther south to the Second Cataract (Great Cataract) during the tenth year of his co-regency. With his massive army, Senusret crushed the

Nubians at Wawat, bringing the territory's wealth under Egyptian control and pressing the captured Nubians into slavery. Upon taking the territory, Senusret I's army began creating a new southern border by erecting forts and strategic outposts, with the express purpose of placing trade routes and Lower Nubia's gold and gemstone mines under Egyptian control.

While no evidence exists of major battles during this time, historians believe that the tribes of Upper Nubia may have begun to be understood as a threat to the Egyptian presence in Lower Nubia. Eight years after establishing a new southern border in Lower Nubia, Senusret I dispatched another expedition into Lower Nubia to further bolster his forces. Senusret I built fortresses and fortifications at Aniba, Buhen, Kor, Ikkur, and Kuban, with his ultimate goal being to create a hard border that would permanently control the movement of goods and services along the Nubian portion of the Nile River, as well as to equip it with so much military might that local provinces and kingdoms would be more apt to fall in line with Egyptian decrees.[69] Kuban, in particular, had a massive military presence since it was designed to protect the gold mines of Wadi Gabgaba and Wadi Allaqi, which flooded the Egyptian treasury with wealth and resources.

---

[69] Edwards, David. (2004). *The Nubian Past: An Archaeology of the Sudan.* Routledge. p 2, 75, 77–78.

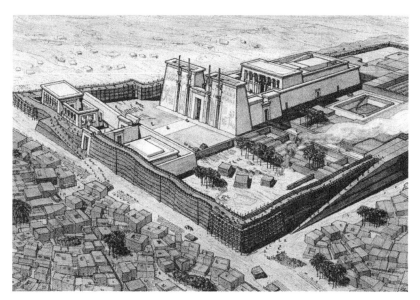

Senusret I would go on to establish thirteen military garrisons in northern Nubia, extending Egypt's border to the Second Cataract, although he established control all the way to the Third Cataract, coming into direct contact with the small Kerma kingdom of Sai. Ordering his general, Mentuhotep, to continue acquiring territory and trade goods, Egypt began sending smaller excursions farther south, sparking tensions throughout the region and indirectly forcing smaller Nubian tribes and villages to align with Kerma for support.

As aggressions rose, however, fate would play an important role in ending Egypt's southern expansion. Papyri letters and tomb remains from the second decade of Senusret I's reign indicate a terrible famine struck Egypt, depleting their food stores and agricultural stability. Soon, in the twentieth year of Senusret I's co-regency, his father, Amenemhat I, died, making Senusret I the sole ruler of Egypt. While literature written years later indicates that Amenemhat I may have been assassinated, what is known is that upon learning of his father's death, Senusret I abandoned his place at the front of the Libyan campaign and returned to his capital city, taking on the mantle of a sole pharaoh.[70]

Upon assuming ownership of the throne, Senusret I continued the small incursions into Upper Nubia but advanced no farther than his already established southernmost fortifications. Instead, Senusret I turned his attention inward, focusing on reestablishing agricultural economics, and he became known for building massive temples, obelisks, and cult centers honoring the god Atum-Ra, utilizing quarried rock and mined gold from Lower Nubia to complete these monuments (a few of which still exist today).[71]

Apparently fearful of potential divisions within his sole reign, Senusret I became widely known for centralizing power by supporting Egyptian officials who supported him and his family. Like his father before him, Senusret I named his son Amenemhat II as co-regent in the fortieth year of his reign. Later, carrying on the traditions of his forefathers, Amenemhat II named his son, Senusret II, as co-regent in 1897 BCE.

And it is here that fate would take an interesting turn.

---

[70] R. B. Parkinson. (1999). *The Tale of Sinuhe and Other Ancient Egyptian Poems.* Oxford World's Classics. p. 21.

[71] Grajetzki, W. (2006). *The Middle Kingdom of Ancient Egypt: History, Archaeology and Society.* Duckworth, London p. 38 - 41.

Senusret II was much like his ancestor, Senusret I. He desired expansion for trade, knowing that the empire could not depend on its internal wealth to survive. He also curried the favor of local officials throughout his kingdom, blessing those who aligned with him with material wealth and positions. Senusret II's reign was known as a time of peace and prosperity, as he also established trade routes throughout the Near East, the Libyan Desert, and Upper Nubia. Like his ancestor, Senusret II became widely known for working toward further centralization of Egyptian power, buying favor with the wealth of the treasury.[72]

In approximately 1890 BCE, foreigners from the east began to visit Egypt en masse. Believed by modern historians to be nomads hailing from the land of Canaan, these Semitic people, led by their leader, Abisha the Hyksos, brought with them tribute for Pharaoh Senusret II and his regents. While Semitic people had been present in Egypt throughout its history and were a major part of its building projects and commerce, this was the first time in recorded history that the

---

[72] Callender, Gae. (2004). "The Middle Kingdom Renaissance (c.2055-1650 BC)." *The Oxford History of Ancient Egypt*. Oxford University Press. p 137-171.

name Hyksos had been used, and with his tribute to Senusret II, Abisha and his people became highly favored among the Egyptian aristocracy. The Hyksos would become a major part of Egypt's culture for the next two hundred years, serving as settled soldiers in its military, house workers, trade workers, and eventually as government officials in important areas such as Memphis and Avaris.[73]

Soon, the Hyksos would bring Egypt to its knees, all with the aid of the Kingdom of Kerma.

Classic Kerma – The Golden Age

Near the end of Amenemhat III's reign in 1814 BCE, Egypt had devolved into regional governments due to inefficient leadership from the pharaoh, with local magistrates beginning to exert greater control over areas under their command. However, with the largest bulk of the military under his control, Amenemhat III continued expeditions into Nubia. Tensions were high along Egypt's southern border, as Kush was now pushing into parts of Lower Nubia and aligning local tribes under their banner. While Egypt's government was beginning to decentralize, the kings of Kerma were consolidating their power and growing their well-trained armies.

With the short reign and death of Amenemhat IV in 1806 BCE, Egypt was thrown into turmoil. Leaving no male heir, Amenemhat III's daughter, Sobekneferu, took the throne. Not raised to reign as a pharaoh (she was the half-sister of Amenemhat IV *and* the younger sister of Neferuptah, her older sister who died at an early age), Sobekneferu was not equipped to handle the needs of a kingdom on the verge of civil war. Within four short years, Sobekneferu was dead, and with no heir, Egypt was plunged into chaos.

---

[73] Bietak, Manfred. (2012). "Hyksos." *The Encyclopedia of Ancient History*. John Wiley & Sons.

As Egypt segmented into regional governments during the weak Thirteenth Dynasty (1803-1649 BCE), the governors of the frontier forts along Egypt's southern borders found their military and powers greatly diminished. After the ten-year reign of Sobekhotep IV (circa 1725), Egypt began to remove its larger garrisons from Nubia to focus on issues within its own borders. Due to this, Kerma quickly swarmed over Egypt's established borders within Lower Nubia and seized control of its mines and quarries. Kerma also took control of Egypt's former fortresses and border forts, taking statues of its gods and royal seals back to their capital city. Many of these spoils of war were uncovered during archaeological excavations of Kerma in the 20th century.[74] With the seizure of Wawat, Kerma's wealth increased exponentially, and the age of Classic Kerma began.

While the Kerma began to take over large swaths of former Egyptian territory, instead of removing all traces of Egyptian culture, evidence suggests that the Kerma began to adopt many aspects of Egyptian culture into their own, including Egyptian burial styles. Graves within Kerma cities reveal a mixture of both Kerma and Egyptian pottery and jewelry, as well as Egyptian-styled statuettes and votives.

With their empire growing, the Kerma kings realized they would soon become ineffective in governing such a large empire. Seeing the issues of Egypt in controlling their territories, Kerma kings began to install loyal governors over different regions. These governors, called pestos, answered only to the king and queen and were to enact decrees that came from their centralized government in Kerma proper. Queens shared the same authority as kings, and throughout Kerma's history, they sometimes held sole authority over the kingdom.

One of the major decrees issued during the Classic Kerma phase was the sole worship of Amun. While worshiped as one of the primary gods in Egypt, in Kerma, Amun was established as the universal god. With a dedication approaching monotheism, government-funded temples could only be dedicated to Amun. While worship of minor local gods could continue in the home, public displays of worship could only be offered to Amun, as Kerma was dedicated solely to him.[75]

---

[74] Edwards, David. (2004). *The Nubian Past: An Archaeology of the Sudan.* Routledge. p 95.

[75] Gabolde, Luc. (2021). *The Amun Cult and Its Development in Nubia.* The Oxford Handbook of Ancient Nubia.

During this time, the Sai kingdom of the Third Cataract became integrated with Kerma. Separated by seven to ten days of travel from the city of Kerma, Sai had risen as a powerful city-state in its own right. However, in joining with the Kingdom of Kerma, Sai was fitted with powerful defenses, even reconstructing its royal palace with fortifications and watchtowers.[76] With the assimilation of Sai, Kerma held all the territory from the Second Cataract to the Fourth Cataract.

And they would soon hold much more.

The Combined Strength of the Hyksos and Kerma

In approximately 1650 BCE, the Hyksos united many of the restless territories of Lower Egypt and took control. Led by Salitis I, the Hyksos quickly secured power and established the first foreign-controlled dynasty of ancient Egypt: the Fifteenth Dynasty. Seeing an opportunity, the king of Kerma (sometimes called Uratrerses by Greek historians) struck an accord with Salitis I and attacked Egypt from the south.

---

[76] Shaunauk. (2019). "What Kerma Implies for the Remains of Sai." 25 July 2021. https://blogs.brown.edu/arch-0760-s01-2019-spring/2019/04/06/what-kerma-implies-for-the-remains-of-sai/.

By the reign of Khyan, the fourth pharaoh of the Hyksos dynasty, the Hyksos were successful in overtaking all of Egypt, pushing the last remaining vestiges of Egyptian authority to the city of Thebes. The empire of Kerma surrounded Thebes to the south and pinned the Egyptians in place, leaving no escape route.

While not much is known from this invasion period of Egypt's history, as the ancient Egyptians of succeeding generations erased much of the evidence from this period, it has recently been discovered that the Kushites plunged much deeper into Egypt than previously believed. Prior to 2003, most historians believed that Kerma had only advanced to the First Cataract at Aswan, expanding their empire at its height from the First to the Fourth Cataract, making Kerma's empire almost equal in size to that of Egypt. In truth, a discovery at a Theban tomb near Thebes revealed that Kerma came perilously close to annihilating Egypt completely.

At a tomb in El Kab in Upper Egypt, twenty-two lines of hieroglyphs revealed that Egypt was dealt defeat after defeat at the hands of the Kerma empire. Found in the tomb of the governor of El Kab, Sobeknakht, the hieroglyphs revealed that the Egyptians "swept over the mountains, over the Nile, without limit."[77]

---

[77] "Tomb reveals Ancient Egypt's humiliating secret." (2003). Daily Times. 25 July 2021.
https://web.archive.org/web/20131105214410/http://www.dailytimes.com.pk/default.asp?page=story_29-7-2003_pg9_1.

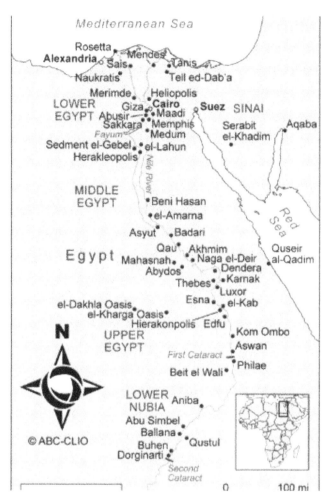

Instead of remaining to occupy the land, however, the empire of Kerma chose to exact tribute upon their seized Egyptian territory, taking gold, statues, alabaster, and slaves. The local Egyptian leaders did not install garrisons upon their newly acquired territory, which still allowed them to maintain a small portion of control. And this would prove to be the eventual undoing of the Kerma empire.

The Fall of Kerma

Circa 1550 BCE, Ahmose I rose to the Theban throne of Egypt. While the Hyksos reigned over Egypt to the north and the Nubians reigned to the south, Ahmose was able to lay claim to the Egyptian throne through his father, Seqenenre Tao II, and brother, Kamose. With his father and brother killed by the Hyksos in battle, Ahmose I was groomed from seven years old to take the Theban throne, and he was known as a charismatic leader.

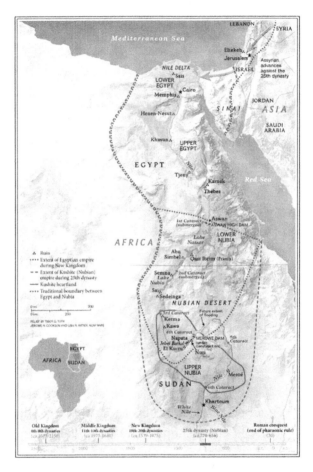

After hiring mercenaries from Nubia and aligning Egyptian villages and cities, Ahmose I forced the Hyksos from the Nile Valley by eventually crushing their capital at Avaris after three prior attempts. Since the Hyksos had established firm trade routes throughout Palestine, their forces soon began to fall back to friendly territory, believing they'd find safety from Egypt. But Ahmose I would allow the Hyksos no respite, even far from Egypt's borders. Ahmose I followed the Hyksos as they retreated, destroying their forts and garrisons in Palestine. His conquest of the Hyksos was complete after he annihilated their fortifications at Sharuhen.[78]

Reestablishing Egyptian control of Lower Egypt, Ahmose I then set about securing the borders of Egypt by launching deeper incursions into Palestine and then along the Nubian border, pushing the forces of Kerma back beyond the Second Cataract. With his borders established, Ahmose set about reorganizing Egypt under the administrative practices of the early Middle Kingdom, demonstrating the learned lessons from the failures of the Twelfth and Thirteenth Dynasties. He reestablished the provinces of Egypt and began to erase the names of the Hyksos and Nubian leaders from Egypt's history, defacing their monuments and reducing their statues to rubble. With the mines and fortresses of Lower Nubia back under Egyptian control, Ahmose I began a number of building projects and laid the foundations of what would become the New Kingdom period of ancient Egypt, which would soon spell the end of the Kingdom of Kerma.

---

[78] Grimal, Nicolas. (1988). *A History of Ancient Egypt*. Librairie Arthéme Fayard. p 192 - 194.

During his first campaign into the Nubian territory, a prince of Kerma named Aata rallied local tribes against Ahmose I's invading army. Upon Aata's defeat against Egypt's overwhelming forces, instead of offering clemency or an opportunity for tribute, Ahmose I had Aata executed. Establishing a new Egyptian outpost at Buhen, Ahmose set about a system of paying local warlords and mercenaries, who then harassed the outer edges of the empire of Kerma. Ahmose also enacted a policy of supporting Nubian princes with gold from the coffers of Wawat, ensuring their loyalty against the Kerma empire.[79] Over the next fifty years, the armies of Egypt would attack Upper Nubia again and again, relentlessly invading its borders to extend its rule and enact vengeance.

In 1500 BCE, in an attempt to mount a rebellion against Egypt's encroachment, Nedjeh, king of Kerma, sought to unite the tribes of Nubia once again. The reigning pharaoh, Thutmose I, traveled up the Nile himself to take part in the battle. Upon reaching Kerma, Thutmose I engaged the forces of Upper Nubia and slaughtered them, personally killing Nedjeh. Tying the king's dead body to the prow of his ship, Thutmose sailed back up the Nile, stopping in every Nubian village along the way to show the people their dead king.[80]

Thutmose would put down three other Nubian rebellions during his reign, going as far as to dredge and widen the First Cataract of the Nile to move troops and supplies into Nubia faster. Thutmose I's crowning achievement during his Nubian campaign was to build a massive fortress at Tombos near the Third Cataract, extending the permanent reach of Egypt deep into the Nubian territory. From Tombos, Thutmose I empowered his local leaders to put down every rebellion at the first hint of trouble and even ordered incursions into Kurgus, the farthest south Egypt had ever reached. Thutmose I would

---

[79] Ibid.

[80] Steindorff, George; Seele, Keith C. (1957). *When Egypt Ruled the East.* University of Chicago Press. p 34.

seek to utterly obliterate every trace of Nubian independence, creating a client state in Nubia that would last over a half millennium.

Chapter 5 – The Kingdom of Kush

Rising from the Ashes of Conquest

Over the next 1,500 years of Nubia's history, the Kingdom of Kush would survive as a vassal state of the Egyptian empire, take control of the Egyptian empire, be challenged by Assyria, and then repel the militarized boot of Rome. Yet, throughout the tumultuous rise and fall of its kingdoms and empires, Egypt and Nubia as a whole continued their cultural exchange, with the Kushite kingdom taking many of the customs of their neighbor yet still remaining a distinct and glorious culture in its own right. Royal marriages were common between the two groups of people, and even Egyptian pharaohs hailed from Nubian descent.

Five hundred years after falling under Egypt's thumb, as Egypt's power began to ebb once again due to the threat of internal and external forces during the late 9th century, the forces of Nubia would rise to topple an empire, establishing the Twenty-fifth Dynasty. The entirety of Egypt would fall under the rule of the Kushite empire. Kushite pharaohs would rule the throne of Egypt, reviving Egypt's practice of temple and monument building, restoring religious traditions, and breathing fresh life into the arts for over a century before being toppled by the Assyrians and forced from Egypt by the eventual establishment of the Twenty-sixth Dynasty of Pharaoh Psamtik I.

After losing control of Egypt, the Kushite kings consolidated their power at the southern Nubian city of Meroe, where the Nubian nobility would begin massive building campaigns of pyramids and palaces. Kushite warrior queens and kings would continue to fight to protect the borders of their empire and dominate the trade routes of central Africa, all while Egypt fell under Hellenistic and then Roman rule. With the arrival of the Greeks in Egypt and the establishment of the Ptolemaic dynasties circa 350 BCE, the Kingdom of Kush again thrived as a regional power. And as Rome conquered Egypt, Kush still grew as an independent power, dominating the movement of goods and controlling the resources of the southern Nile. Over the next 350 years, the armies of Kush would go toe to toe with that of Roman Egypt before succumbing to famine, shifting climates, and the invading forces of the Aksum kingdom in the 4th century CE.

Napata

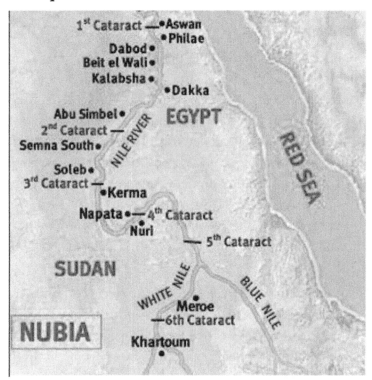

After crushing Kerma in 1504 BCE, Thutmose I knew that if he was to be successful in keeping the Kingdom of Kush as a client state, then Egypt would need to establish permanent Egyptian settlements deep in the Nubian territory. After annexing Nubia and bringing the region under his control, Thutmose I's armies advanced past the Fourth Cataract and constructed the frontier outpost of Kurgus to establish Egyptian control.

While Thutmose I was successful in establishing fortifications throughout Lower and Upper Nubia, rebellions were still common. Local leaders challenged the invading armies of the Egyptians but were quickly put down and forced into slavery. The pharaoh's armies were taking no chances. They had learned from past mistakes in allowing local leaders to administrate their own people, so Egypt installed their own governmental rulers. With the continual threat of forced slavery over their heads and with no central Nubian power, the tribes of the former Kerma empire had no choice but to welcome the Egyptian forces. However, as Egyptian culture continued to mingle with that of Nubia, Kerma's culture began to slowly disappear. What rose in its place was a culture that was distinctly Nubian yet had deep ties to Egyptian life.

Fifty years later, under Thutmose III, the Egyptian empire covered more terrain than at any point in its history. Thutmose III, who served as pharaoh from the age of two, believed it was his divine destiny to reign over all the known world and expanded his territory from Syria to below the Fourth Cataract in ancient Nubia, putting down rebellions and consolidating power. In Nubia, Thutmose III desired to establish a thoroughly Egyptian city deep within the heart of the client state. Knowing that injecting Egyptian customs and culture into a conquered territory would create permanent change more than simple military might, Thutmose III began a campaign of placing religious and administrative settlements along the Nubian Nile. Settling on the southernmost point of his extended kingdom, Thutmose III established the city of Napata, and soon, Napata would rise to become the administrative and religious capital of Kush.

While earlier Egyptian kingdoms had recognized Swenett and Elephantine as the source of the Nile and its annual inundation, therefore being responsible for creation and regeneration, the Egyptians soon came to look at the southernmost city of their newly acquired Nubian empire as

holy. Focusing their attention on a massive flat-topped rock that stood in the center of the Napata settlement named Jebel Barkal, the priests of Egypt claimed that the hill was the home of the Egyptian and Nubian god Amun. Since the Nile was now known to be birthed from around the upper cataracts near Napata rather than the cataract at Aswan, it made sense to the Egyptians that their primary god had been born at this location. Therefore, it was the birthplace of royal rule, as all pharaohs were descended from and gained their right to rule from Amun himself (because of this, later Kushite pharaohs of Egypt during the 8th century BCE would claim their right to rule due to this belief).

Yet, while Napata became known as one of Egypt's new primary religious cult centers, Napata's true strength was in its gold and incense production.[81] Due to advances in mining techniques and the conquest of Upper Nubian territory and their inroads throughout Palestine due to the defeat of the Hyksos, Egypt began to mine so much gold near Napata that they became the largest producer of gold throughout Asia Minor and the Mediterranean.[82] However, in order to mine more gold, workers were needed. Under the reign of the Egyptians, rebellious Nubians would be pressed into forced service to work the mines. The conditions were so brutal and the mortality rate so high that the great historian Diodorus of Sicily wrote of the horrid

---

[81] Cusick, James. (2015). *Studies in Culture Contact: Interaction, Culture Change, and Archaeology*. SIU Press. p 269.

[82] Ibid; p. 269 – 274.

Nubian gold mines in his *Bibliotheca historica*, which would later inspire the works of Karl Marx.[83]

While conditions may have been severe for slaves and the rebels during Egypt's occupation of Nubia, the nobility and royal families of Kush enjoyed a much loftier status. These Nubians were important members of Egyptian society and were deeply respected by Egyptian authorities. The deified royal queen, sister, and mother Ahmose-Nefertari is believed by numerous historians to have been Nubian, as she was depicted as having black skin.[84] To the Egyptians, black skin symbolized rebirth and resurrection, representing the life-giving black silt of the Nile that comes with the river's yearly inundation. It was uncommon for living people in Egyptian society to be depicted with jet black skin; however, all of Ahmose-Nefertari's depictions show her in this light, leading scholars to believe she bore the black skin of the Nubians. Furthermore, evidence suggests that her father, Seqenenre Tao, was Nubian, as an examination of his mummy has revealed he had the genetically tightly curled hair and features of Upper Kushites.

During the Twenty-fourth Dynasty of Egypt, Nubian officials began to rise into essential positions within Egypt. During the occupation of Kush, it was a common practice for the children of Nubian nobility to be sent to Egypt for education. This would allow the children to be raised with Egyptian customs and culture, ensuring loyalty to the pharaonic throne. As the children became adults, they would be returned to Kush to serve as government officials, serving as priests, dignitaries, and emissaries. While commoners could serve in minor positions, all positions of power within Kush were held by those who had been raised in the Egyptian court.[85]

---

[83] Marx, Karl (2008). [1867]. Capital. OUP. p 151.

[84] Bernal, Martin. (1987). "Black Athena: Afroasiatic Roots of Classical Civilization." *The Fabrication of Ancient Greece, 1785 - 1985, Vol. I.* Rutgers University Press.

[85] Torok, László. (1998). *The Kingdom of Kush: Handbook of the Napatan-Civilization.* Leiden: BRILL. pp. 132-133, 153-184.

The Viceroys of Kush

During Egypt's occupation of Kush and then later throughout Kush's reign over the Egyptian empire, Egypt appointed administrators called viceroys over Kush. Due to the amount of gold being mined throughout the Kushite kingdom, the viceroy of Kush was a hallowed position and was titled the King's Son, which was an honor that continued into the afterlife. The viceroy of Kush, in turn, had two deputies that served under him, one administering Egypt's policies over Wawat (the largest producer of gold in Lower Nubia) and one governing Kush.[86] Viceroys were ultimately responsible for the goings-on within the Kingdom of Kush, even handling military Meroitic aspects of Egypt's occupation of the territory.[87]

---

[86] "Viceroy of Kush." (2020). Tour Egypt. 28 July 2021. http://www.touregypt.net/viceroyofkush.htm.

[87] Abbas, Mohamed Raafat. (2018). *Historical Observations on the Military Role of Three Ramesside Viceroys of Kush.* ENIM. 28 July 2021. http://www.enim-egyptologie.fr/revue/2018/4/Abbas_ENiM11_p33-40.swf.pdf.

The viceroys of Kush held so much power in ancient Egypt that during the Ramesside reign in the 10th century BCE, a near civil war broke out between the high priest of Thebes and the Kushite viceroy, Panehesy, who was a Nubian. The high priest of Amun of Thebes, Amenhotep, ruled with the power of a king over Upper Egypt. The viceroy of Kush held power over Nubia and the gold production of the southern empire. As both men vied for control, skirmishes and disagreements were common along the border, leading to the plundering of tombs and monuments throughout the southern Egyptian empire.

The viceroy of Kush was then charged by Rameses XI with administering control over the granaries of southern Egypt, placing him in control of the military. Panehesy then set about using the military to enact near martial law over Thebes, leading to a revolt led by Amenhotep against the occupying force. In 1082, witnessing the weakening of Thebes, Rameses XI ordered soldiers to the defense of the high priest, yet Panehesy continued his aggression, eventually forcing Amenhotep from Thebes. Acknowledging that he now had a full-scale revolt on his hands, Rameses XI stripped Panehesy of his title and assembled his northern army to force the former viceroy from Egypt. Rameses XI ordered new leadership in Thebes, naming Herihor as the high priest and Paiankh as the viceroy of Kush. Paiankh and Herihor would continue to wage war against Panehesy, who set up a private kingdom within Lower Nubia that he would control until his natural death years later. The descendants of Herihor would go on to rule as pharaoh, and Paiankh's children would eventually take up positions of high nobility within the kingdom.[88]

---

[88] Torok, László. (1998). The Kingdom of Kush: Handbook of the Napatan-Meroitic Civilization. Leiden: BRILL. pp. 132-133, 153-184.

From Kingdom to Empire: Kush Rises Again
The Napatan Empire

As Egypt once again felt the strain from its internal turmoil, its hold on its territories began to weaken. The year 1075 BCE is the scholarly agreed endpoint of Egypt's New Kingdom period. During this time, Egypt's hold on neighboring countries, such as Syria, Palestine, and Nubia, essentially ceased.

As the New Kingdom of Egypt fell apart, Kush once again became independent, establishing Napata as its capital. No longer having to supply Egypt with its own internal resources, the kings of Napata set about reestablishing trade and commerce with surrounding kingdoms and establishing taxes and social goods within Nubia, soon overtaking Egypt as the central power of northeast Africa.

The kings of Kush would rule from the city of Napata, wielding control over the region's territorial kings and princes and the people under their care. The Kushite kings embarked upon building projects that rivaled that of their neighbor to the north and would establish bureaucratic and religious policies that would establish Kush as a major empire in North Africa's history.

While Napata was the capital, the Nubian territory of El-Kurru held a place of high importance within the Kushite kingdom. Home to one of the largest necropolises of ancient Nubia, El-Kurru was originally settled during the time of the Kerma. The city of El-Kurru was central to Kush's gold trade, and it was surrounded by mines and areas for gold refinement. The land surrounding El-Kurru was conducive to farming, enabling the city to support greater populations and making it an important trading location. During the 9th century BCE, burials at the site became marked with structures like those of the New Kingdom of Egypt, with temple enclosures and small interior areas for offerings. The site of El-Kurru was so important to the Kushite kingdom that it would become the final resting place of the founder of Egypt's Twenty-fifth Dynasty, Prince Alara of Kush, as well as his successor, King Kashta, the eventual ruler of the combined Kushite and Egyptian state. Also located within the necropolises of El-Kurru were Alara's sister, the priestess of Amun, and Kashta's daughter, Princess Amenirdis I. Like earlier Nubian kingdoms, during the time of Kush's Napata empire, women held high positions of honor and were esteemed leaders.

As Kush was now no longer a vassal state of Egypt, practices had to be put in place to establish the authority of the Kushite kings and queens while also stabilizing the kingdom with its blended Egyptian and Kushite cultures. The priestess of Amun during the time of Prince Alara was responsible for blending the Egyptian principles of kingship with the practices and traditions of the Kushite empire and teaching them to the serving nobility. Princess Amenirdis would wear the title of God's Wife of Amun Elect and would serve as Divine

Adoratrice, essentially meaning the governor of Upper Egypt, while serving under King Kashta.[89]

As the influence of Kush grew, the empire began to overtake governmental positions of Upper Egypt. During Egypt's weak Twenty-third Dynasty (circa 837 BCE), the Egyptian pharaoh's power had weakened so significantly that he withdrew completely from Thebes and retreated to Het-Nepsut in northern Egypt. King Kashta, seeing his chance to take the kingdom of Egypt without a fight, marched with his armies north and soon declared himself the king of both Upper and Lower Egypt. This would plant the seeds of Kush's famed Twenty-fifth Dynasty, also known as the Nubian Dynasty, and the time of the Black Pharaohs.

The Twenty-fifth Dynasty – The Reign of the Black Pharaohs

Piye, like his father Kashta before him, saw an opportunity in the weakness of Egypt's leaders. Not content to rule from Thebes and Lower Egypt in name only, Piye desired to truly rule over the entirety of Egypt and Kush. Beginning in the 740s BCE, Piye began to send incursions into Lower Egypt, testing the rule and strength of its northern leaders.

---

[89] Torok, László. (1998). The Kingdom of Kush: Handbook of the Napatan-Meroitic Civilization. Leiden: BRILL. pp. 132-133, 153-184.

The local kings of Lower Egypt and the Nile Delta, including Tefnakht of Sais and Nimlot of Khmunu, united to respond to Piye's growing influence. Raising an army to march south to Hershef (Herakleopolis), they sought to take command of the city and cripple Piye's advance north. The city's king, Peftjauawybast, was loyal to the Nubian pharaoh, and the kings of Lower Egypt believed if they could remove the local king and install a king loyal to them, they would retake control of Middle Egypt and gain a foothold to invade Thebes. Upon learning of the advancing army from the north, the king of Hershef sent an appeal for aid to Piye, and Piye would answer with a show of force not seen in Lower Egypt since the days of the Hyksos.

Piye assembled his army and calvary, also calling in mercenaries from the edges of the Nubian kingdom, and marched for Hershef. However, instead of inspiring his army to march for the glory of his empire, Piye believed that he was leading a religious war. Believing that he was the incarnation of Atum and the servant of Amun, Piye believed the rival kings were sowing discord and unrighteousness; therefore, they were in violation of *maat*, the guiding philosophy of ancient Egypt representing righteousness and justice. Piye believed that in rising against him, the rival kings were in violation of the universal laws that held up Egyptian society, so he charged his soldiers to ritually cleanse themselves, to fast, and to pray before beginning their march and assault on Lower Egypt.[90]

---

[90] Draper, Robert. (2008). "The Black Pharaohs." *National Geographic Magazine.*

Piye's army utterly annihilated the opposing kings of Lower Egypt, and Piye recorded his victory in his Victory Stele, writing,

> Hear what I have done in exceeding the ancestors. I am the king, the representation of god, the living image of Atum, who issued from the womb marked as ruler, who is feared by those greater than he, [whose father] knew and whose mother perceived even in the egg that he would be ruler, the good god, beloved of the gods, the Son of Ra, who acts with his two arms, Piye, beloved of Amun

-Victory Stele of Piye

The cities of Hershef, Khmunu (Hermopolis), and Memphis all fell to the pharaoh's army, and King Nimlot, Iuput II of Onu, and Osorkon IV of Djanet swore fealty to Piye, establishing him as the ruler of Upper and Lower Egypt. Piye took the names Usimare and Sneferre, symbolizing his rule over all of Egypt. His main opponent, Tefnakht, refused to pay homage to Piye but acknowledged him as pharaoh. He retreated to a small island in the Nile Delta and set up his own kingdom, rarely interfering in the later affairs of Egypt. Now ruler over the entirety of Egypt and Kush, Piye established Peftjauawybast as his vassal at Hershef to administrate his decrees throughout Lower Egypt and then returned to his homelands of Napata and El-Kurru, never setting foot in Egypt again. The kings of Egypt, now united under the rulership of Piye, were free to administrate their kingdoms as they wished.[91]

Piye's rule would represent a harkening back to the Egypt of yore, with a focus on the arts, religious influence, and building projects, such as the construction of pyramids and temples. Piye is credited with establishing the first Nubian pyramid within El-Kurru at the royal necropolis. Utilizing modern Nubian practices to build the pyramid, resulting in a narrower base and steeper incline than Egyptian pyramids of the Old and Middle Kingdoms, Piye's pyramid lent a distinct appearance to the pyramids of Kush that would blend the two cultures of the empire together in a way that was designed to last for eternity. Piye also improved on existing Egyptian temples by adding columned forecourts, a feature of Nubian architecture. The best example of this is the Temple of Amun at Jebel Barkal, which, during the Twenty-fifth Dynasty, represented the spiritual heart of the combined Kushite and Egyptian empire. This would inspire future rulers of the Kushite empire to continue to blend the cultures of

---

[91] Herodotus. (2003). *The Histories*. Penguin Books. p 106–107, 133–134.

Egypt and Kush, such as using Egyptian writing, adopting customs from Egypt, and using secondary Egyptian names.[92]

In 712 BCE, Shebitku (Shabataka), nephew of King Piye, assumed the throne upon Piye's death and immediately led an assault upon the kings of the Nile Valley. Resisting the authority of the Nubian king, Tefnakht's son, Bocchoris of Sais, led a rebellion with a coalition of kings throughout Lower Egypt. King Shebitku mounted an invasion of

---

[92] Torok, Lazlo. (1998). *The Kingdom of Kush: Handbook of the Napatan-Meroitic Civilization.* Leiden. P 132-133,153-184.

the northern territories and, like his predecessor, crushed the coalition of rebellious kings. Instead of allowing his nemesis to escape, however, Shebitku had Bocchoris brought before him and burned alive. After putting down the rebellion of the northern kings once and for all, Shebitku moved the capital of Egypt from Thebes to Memphis.

It is during the reign of Shebitku that the Kingdom of Kush would begin to have run-ins with the empire of Assyria. Evidence exists of positive interactions between Shebitku and Sargon II, with Sargon II's scribes referring to Shebitku's extradition of an Assyrian fugitive, Iamani of Ashdod.[93] However, within a few short years, Shebitku would support a rebellion against Assyria by the Philistines at Ashdod. While Egypt and the Philistines were defeated at Ashdod by the Assyrian armies, this would be the beginning of intergenerational battles between the rulers of Kush and Assyria, as Sargon II would not soon forget the slight of Egypt defending Sargon II's enemy. And fifty years later, Ashurbanipal, Sargon II's great-grandson, would march upon Egypt and bring an end to the Kushite rule.

Under King Shabaqo (ruling from 707 to 690 BCE and sometimes confused with the reign of Shebitku), Egypt entered a period of religious fervor not seen for hundreds of years. Shabaqo, like his predecessors, believed that like the pharaohs of old, he was descended from the gods and destined to rule over the great empire. Pharaoh Shabaqo had himself ritually ordained as the high priest of Amun, bringing together the crown and the priesthood and giving himself unlimited power in the eyes of Egyptian and Kushite society.

However, it would be King Taharqa, son of Piye, that would bring about the Twenty-fifth Dynasty's golden age and represent the height of power for the Kushite empire.

---

[93] Torok, Lazlo. (1998). *The Kingdom of Kush: Handbook of the Napatan-Meroitic Civilization.* Leiden. P 132-133,153-184.

Taharqa

Unlike his father, who chose to rule from Nubia, upon taking the combined throne of Kush and Egypt, Taharqa chose to rule from the city of Djanet, located upon the Nile Delta. Crowned at Memphis in 690 BCE, like his predecessors, Taharqa believed that he was favored by the god Amun and destined to reign over the combined empires of North Africa. Taharqa flooded the coffers of the temples of Amun throughout the empire, taking on the role of his predecessor as high priest of Amun. During Taharqa's time as pharaoh, the Nile was blessed with an abundance of yearly flooding and, therefore, land fertility, leading to the storehouses of Egypt and Nubia being filled with crops and wine. Known as a time of prosperity not seen since the Middle Kingdom, Taharqa's reign was the height of the Kushite empire.[94]

Taharqa continued the massive building projects of his father, importing famed cedar from Lebanon to outfit temples and monuments at Karnak, Thebes, Qasr Ibrim, and, of course, Jebel Barkal, which had become the holiest site of the empire. As the priest of Amun, the kings of the Twenty-fifth Dynasty claimed their right to rule came from Amun's original home upon the hill of Jebel Barkal, which, therefore, destined the Nubian kings with the right to rule over the combined kingdom. Taharqa would pour vast amounts of wealth into the construction of monuments at Jebel Barkal, as well as improvements to the temples of Karnak. At Nuri, Taharqa designed his own pyramid, the largest of ancient Nubia, and had a tomb cut into the surrounding stone for worship and offerings.

While Taharqa is primarily known to historians as the Nubian pharaoh who brought about a renaissance of art and monument building throughout Egypt, Taharqa's military campaigns throughout the ancient world were equally as impressive. Under Taharqa's reign, the armies of Kush defeated kingdoms throughout the Near East and North Africa, including that of the Libyans, Phoenicians, and Palestinians. The Old Testament in 2 Kings 19:9 and Isaiah 37:9 both mentions the forces of Taharqa assisting King Hezekiah to repel the Assyrian armies from Judah. The forces of Egypt, including Nubian infantry and most notably Nubian archers, prevented Assyria from taking Jerusalem, even though Taharqa's military suffered grievous casualties. However, since Assyria's forces were crippled and their supply lines decimated, Assyria was forced to retreat and abandoned Judah.[95] Assyria would attempt to retake portions of Lebanon over the

---

[94] Welsby, Derek. (1996). *The Kingdom of Kush*. British Museum Press. p 169.
[95] Aubin, Henry. (2002). *The Rescue of Jerusalem*. Soho Press, Inc. p 155.

next twenty years, primarily at Khor, but was forced to pay tribute to Taharqa, enriching Taharqa's building projects in the city of Kawa.

Yet, the reign of the Black Pharaohs would not be rid of Assyria so easily. Upon the assassination of Assyria's emperor, Sennacherib, a rebellion broke out within the Assyrian empire. Assyria was eventually brought under control by Sennacherib's son, Esarhaddon, and it would unite to invade Egypt and force Taharqa from power. From 679 to 678 BCE, Assyria marched upon towns loyal to Egypt within Palestine and destroyed Sidon, forcing entire regions to pay tribute to Assyria. In 674 BCE, with their expanded borders and supply lines fortified and secured, the Assyrian army flooded Lower Egypt. Again, however, Taharqa was able to push back the invading army and forced the Assyrians from Khor, entering into an alliance with the king of Tyre, Ba'lu. In 671 BCE, Esarhaddon chose to lead his armies himself and broke through Kush's allies and buffer territories.[96] Within the year, Assyria laid siege to Memphis and conquered Lower Egypt. However, instead of remaining in Memphis, Esarhaddon

---

[96] Welsby, Derek. (1996). *The Kingdom of Kush*. British Museum Press. p 169.

returned to Syria, enacting harsh tribute upon the kings of Lower Egypt.

Taharqa's kingdom was now bereft of a third of its territory and weary of war, but he again mustered an army to march north. In 669 BCE, Taharqa retook Memphis and Lower Egypt and destroyed Assyria's outposts and fortifications. In response, Esarhaddon brought his forces to bear. This time, however, fate would not be on Taharqa's side. In 668 BCE, Esarhaddon died, and his rule passed to his son, Ashurbanipal. Charismatic and well-educated, Ashurbanipal had been schooled on military tactics from infancy. A great deal of Ashurbanipal's education was spent learning the craft of spymastery and espionage, and Assyria's new ruler would utilize this knowledge during his conquest of Egypt.[97] Placing spies throughout Egypt, Ashurbanipal began to sow discontent concerning Taharqa's reign with the kings of the Nile Delta. With loyalties weakened, the Assyrian army marched through Egypt, securing Thebes within a year, and forced the Nubian forces from Egypt. In turn, Assyria established vassal kings in every major city throughout Egypt, tightening their control over their expanded empire.

Defeated, Taharqa abandoned Egypt and was entombed beneath his pyramid at Nuri in 664 BCE.

The Fall of Napata

Upon Taharqa's retreat and the collapse of the combined Nubian and Egyptian empire, the Nubian prince Tantamani assumed control of the city of Napata. Desiring to retake control of southern Egypt as his first step of reestablishing the empire, Tantamani sailed with his army to Thebes. Upon arrival, Tantamani stated that the royal temples and cults had been desecrated, and using this as motivation, his armies forced the Assyrians from Thebes. His forces proclaimed Tantamani as the king of Egypt and soon set out to retake Egypt for the Kushite empire.

---

[97] Ibid.

In 665 BCE, Tantamani's armies moved north along the Nile until they arrived at Memphis. There, Tantamani executed Assyria's vassal king, Necho I, and forced his son, Psamtik I, to flee. With Upper Egypt now solidified under his control, Tantamani marched upon the cities of Lower Egypt, bringing them back under the banner of Kush.

However, Tantamani's victory would be short-lived. In 664 BCE, Psamtik I returned to Egypt with Ashurbanipal and his armies, their ranks freshly filled with mercenaries from Anatolia. Unable to withstand the might of Assyria's military, Tantamani abandoned Lower Egypt and fled to Thebes. However, Psamtik I would not let the execution of his father remain unavenged. Assyria's army sacked Thebes, crushing the city and executing its inhabitants. Tantamani barely escaped and fled via the Nile to Nubia, never entering Egypt again. In 663 BCE, Ashurbanipal set Psamtik I upon the throne of Lower Egypt. However, within a few short years, Psamtik I united the kings of Egypt under his strong rule, forcing even Assyria from Egypt. Psamtik I would then take control of Thebes, again unifying Egypt solely under Egyptian control for the first time in over a century.

While Tantamani would never again enter Egypt during his life, nor would Kushite kings reign over Egypt again, the rulers of the Kushite empire would continue to claim their rightful reign over their northern neighbor for over fifty years and rule from their capital city of Napata. After Tantamani's death, he was entombed in the royal necropolis of El-Kurru and succeeded by Taharqa's son, Atlanersa. But it would be Atlanersa's successor, Aspelta, who would witness Napata's abandonment, as Egypt's new pharaohs would seek retribution for years of Kushite rule.

In Egypt, the pharaohs of the Twenty-sixth Dynasty set about erasing the history of the Kushite occupation of Egypt. Defacing the monuments of the Nubian kings, Psamtik II set about a program of destroying all records of the Nubian pharaohs and nobility. In 593 BCE, Psamtik II ordered incursions into Kush to prepare the way for his invasion force. In 592 BCE, the armies of Egypt sacked the city of Napata, forcing the armies of Kush to abandon the city and bringing an end to Napata's complete control over the Kush empire.

Meroe

In 590 BCE, after the Kush army had abandoned Napata, the city of Meroe found itself as the new future capital of the Kush empire. Founded in 800 BCE and located along the Nile near the modern-day city of Shendi, Meroe was strategically located to control trade from central Africa to the Mediterranean Sea. Herodotus proclaimed Meroe as "the mother city of other Ethiopians," and the nobility of

Meroe would control over 620 miles of territory north to south along the Nile, and at its height, it would control 932 miles east to west.[98]

What historians refer to as Meroe was actually formed from three different cities: Naqa, Meroe, and Musawwarat es-Sufra. Together, these three cities formed the Island of Meroe, and it would become a powerful kingdom that outlasted the Persian influence of Egypt, the Ptolemaic reign of Egypt, and Rome's dominance of northeastern Africa. While Nubian kings and queens would continue to base their legitimacy as the pharaoh of Egypt upon their temple at Jebel Barkal, Nubians would never again reign on the throne of Egypt. However, Kushite royalty would continue to have powerful sway and influence upon the cultures of northeastern Africa and dominate trade throughout the region, even controlling the flow of gold, ivory, and slaves to the Roman Empire from central Africa.

From 590 BCE to circa 300 BCE, while the queens and kings of Kush ruled from Meroe, the priests of Jebel Barkal controlled the Kushite religion from Napata. Since Amun was the only god that was allowed to be worshiped publicly throughout Kush, the priests of Amun arguably held as much power over Kush as the royal families. Partially deciphered Meroitic texts reveal an extended power struggle between the kings and high priests of Napata, and according to the historian Diodorus Siculus, in 300 BCE, the Kushite king Ergamenes had the priests of Napata executed.[99]

While it is quite probable that there was no Kushite king named Ergamenes, as Ergamenes is not a Nubian name, the first Kushite king officially buried at Meroe was King Arkamani, who may have been to who Diodorus was referring. While the necropolis of Meroe had been in use for some time, it was Arkamani's burial that influenced all royal

---

[98] Adams, William Y. (1977). *Nubia: Corridor to Africa.* Princeton University Press. p. 302.

[99] Fage, J. D; Roland, Anthony O. (1979). *The Cambridge History of Africa.* Cambridge University Press. p 228.

burials to be shifted to Meroe from Napata and Jebel Barkal, establishing Meroe and its leaders as the true seat of power of Kush. Also during this time, evidence of the public worship of gods other than Amun surfaced. Other gods of Egypt, such as Bast (the Egyptian goddess in the form of the black panther), were widely popular. However, in Meroe, a number of other myths developed with gods that were not of the Egyptian pantheon but were syncretically added in, such as the worship of the child of Bast, Apedemak.[100]

While no longer rulers over the combined Egyptian and Kush empire, the people of Meroe carried on many Egyptian traditions and customs, including a focus on burials and the afterlife. It is during the Meroitic period that the pyramids of Sudan, which still stand today, were birthed. Kings and queens were entombed within complex burial chambers beneath steep pyramids with seventy-degree slopes. However, in Meroe, pyramid tombs and ornate burials were common even among the lesser nobility, leading to a building explosion within its necropolis.

---

[100] Claude, Traunecker. (2001). *The Gods of Egypt (1st English Language Edition, Enhanced and Expanded Edition)*. Cornell University Press. p. 106.

The Kingdom of Meroe, while primarily rural like the other Nubian kingdoms before it, was not a backwater trading post. The cities that made up Meroe were ancient industrial centers whose sources of wealth moved beyond Nubia's earlier past of mining gold and precious metals for metalworking and trade. Archaeological evidence shows that much of Kush's wealth during its Meroitic period came from the production of iron for use in tools and weapons. The queens and kings of Meroe directly controlled the flow of goods that went into its metal production, as well as administrating the exportation of goods through pricing and trade. Tools and weapons manufactured by Meroitic Kush have been found as far away as China, with trade routes set up through modern-day Afghanistan, Pakistan, and India.[101]

One of the most striking advances of the Kushite empire was the development of its own written language. Ancient Nubia, until circa 300 BCE, did not have its own written language (at least not one that has been discovered). However, by 300 BCE, evidence demonstrates that the city of Meroe had developed separate languages for record-keeping and stone inscriptions. The language for record-keeping, called Meroitic Cursive, was written on Egyptian papyrus or clay with a stylus of metal, bone, or ivory. Meroitic Hieroglyphic was used for tombs, royal stelae, or religious inscriptions. Both languages have yet to be fully deciphered, as there are very few bilingual comparison documents or inscriptions. The use of the Meroitic language declined in the early 4th century with the fall of Kush to the Kingdom of Aksum and the conquest of the Nobatae people. The last known use of Meroitic Cursive was in a religious decree dated to the 5th century, and by the 6th century, the spoken Meroitic language is assumed to have

---

[101] Stofferahn, Steven; Wood, Sarah. (2016). *Lecture 30: Ancient Africa [CLCS 181: Classical World Civilizations]*. Purdue University, School of Languages and Cultures.

been supplanted with that of Byzantine Greek and the language classified as Old Nubian.[102]

During Meroe's height of power, the city of Musawwarat es-Sufra, constructed in 300 BCE, played an important role in the evolution of the Meroitic kingdom and was potentially the seat of power of the famous Nubian queens Amanirenas, Amanishakheto, Nawidemak, and Amanitore. Musawwarat es-Sufra is an archaeological masterpiece, and it was constructed differently than any other city within the Kushite empire or Egypt. While the exact purpose of a number of buildings in the site remains unknown, there are three distinct features of the city: the Great Reservoir, the Great Enclosure, and the Temple of the Lion. The Great Reservoir was a water catchment basin with a circular wall, running over 820 feet and 20 feet deep with several channels that ran directly into it from throughout the city complex. This enabled the reservoir to catch and hold the rainfall from the increasingly short rainy seasons for use throughout the year.[103] The Great Enclosure, considered the main structure of the site, is an archaeological mystery. The labyrinthine structure measures over 480,000 square feet and is a maze of temples, walls, courtyards, columns, small reservoirs, and hallways. Historians have theorized that the Great Enclosure served as an early university, hospital, religious center, and even an area to train elephants. Also in the 3rd century, the thirty-seventh king of Kush, King Arnekhamani, constructed the Temple of the Lion and dedicated it to Apedemak, the son of Bast and Sekhmet. Within the temple complex are

---

[102] Miller, Catharine; Khalil, Mokhtar. (2008). *Multilingualism in Nubia - Old Nubian and Language Uses in Nubia*. Égypte/Monde arabe, Première série. p 27-28.

[103] Claudia Näser. (2006). *The Great Hafir at Musawwarat as-Sufra. Fieldwork of the Archaeological Mission of Humboldt University Berlin in 2005 and 2006. Between the Cataracts. Proceedings of the 11th Conference of Nubian Studies.* Polish Centre of Mediterranean Aerchaeology University of Warsaw, PAM Supplement Series 2.2./1-2.

Egyptian hieroglyphs and depictions of Apedemak with three heads, ruling as the god of Musawwarat es-Sufra.[104]

The Kandakes – Queen Mothers of Nubia

The Kushite empire was unique in that its kings were determined by matrilineal succession. The Kandake, also known as Candace, was the eldest sister of the king of Kush. The eldest sister would bear the next heir after the king, which meant that the Kandake served as a queen mother.

Between 260 BCE and 320 CE, Kandakes would take a central role in the wars, expansion efforts, and trade of the Kushite empire. During this time, sixteen Kandakes of Meroe would serve as outright rulers or queen regents, demonstrating the power women held in Nubian society.

In tomb illustrations, the Kandakes of Meroe were not depicted with Egyptian imagery, quite unlike the tomb depictions of men. Kandakes were depicted as strictly Nubian, with shawls and cloaks over their shoulders and covering their bodies. They were also usually

---

[104] Ferrandino, Gilda; Lorenzini, Matteo. (2015) *3-D Reconstruction of the Lion Temple at Musawwarat es Sufra: 3D model and domain ontologies; in: The Kushite World.* Proceedings of the 11th International Conference for Meroitic Studies, Vienna. 1–4.

depicted alone and in the foreground, such as the Dream Stele of Tantamani from Jebel Barkal.

Tombs of Meroitic Kandakes have been found throughout the three major cities of Meroe and even in Egypt's Abydos. The tomb of Queen Qalhata of the Napatan empire stands next to that of kings at El-Kurru, and at Nuri, the tombs of queens occupy the sacred western plateau with stelae and inscriptions describing the lines of matrilineal succession.[105]

Some of the more well-known Kandakes are:

- Shanakdakhete (r. circa 170 BCE-unknown) - Believed to be the first queen who ruled independent of male influence, Shanakdakhete was often depicted wearing the dress of a warrior, as well as serving as the high priest of Amun.
- Amanirenas (r. circa 40-9 BCE) - Arguably the most famous of the feared Kandakes, Amanirenas is known as the Kandake who went toe to toe with ancient Rome. Known to Rome as the "One-Eyed Queen," Amanirenas conducted Kushite raids as far as Aswan, seizing statues of Augustus Caesar and other Roman officials and returning victorious to Kush. In response, Governor Petronius invaded Napata and razed the city; however, instead of surrendering, Amanirenas attacked Petronius's forces and forced them to retreat to the negotiation table, where Kush and Rome entered into a trade partnership. As part of the negotiations, she returned all of Rome's statuary, with the exception of the head of Caesar, which she buried under the steps of the temple of Amun so people would walk upon the head of Augustus daily.

---

[105] Mark, Joshua. (2018). "The Candaces of Meroe." World History.org. 30 July 2021. https://www.worldhistory.org/The_Candaces_of_Meroe/.

- Amanishakheto (r. circa 10 BCE-2 CE) - Due to damage caused by the infamous tomb raider Giuseppe Ferlini, not much is known of Amanishakheto other than that she was a powerful, independent queen. Ferlini destroyed her tomb with bomb blasts in his search for treasure.
- Amanitore (r. circa 2 -25 CE) - Amanitore rebuilt much of what Rome destroyed at Napata, such as the Temple of Amun, and updated the Temple of Amun at Meroe. During the time of Amanitore, blast furnaces for increased iron production were built throughout Meroe, and trade was established with China. Amanitore reigned during what is considered Meroe's most wealthy period, as Rome became a primary exporter of Kushite iron and agricultural goods.
- Amantitere (r. circa 25 -40 CE) - Amantitere was an independent queen believed to have been mentioned in the Bible in Acts 8:27.
- Amanikhatashan (r. circa 62 -84 CE) - Amanikhatashan was an ally of Rome during Rome's war with Palestine in 66 CE, supplying the Caesar with Kushite cavalry and bowmen
- Maleqorobar (r. 266-283 CE) - Few records remain of this independent queen; however, it is during Maleqorobar's reign that trade with Rome began to wane. Evidence suggests there was a decline in land fertility around Meroe at this time, presumably from over-farming, climate change, and other factors.

- Lahideamani (r. circa 306-314 CE) - Lahideamani bears the distinction as the last known Queen Mother of Kush. By 315 BCE, Meroe had completely lost its trade partnership with Rome, with Rome now favoring the Kingdom of Aksum in Ethiopia. Due to over-farming and forest depletion, as the forests were used to create fuel for Meroe's iron industry, Meroe's trade sank to a historic low. By 350 CE, Meroe would be completely abandoned.[106]

Meroe's Interactions with Rome

After Egypt fell to Roman rule in 30 BCE, Rome turned its eyes to the wealthy Kingdom of Kush to the south. At Philae, Rome invited the local kings and queens to the negotiation table in order to set up client states throughout the region and define the borders of southern Egypt. And while historians debate the cause of the future conflict between Rome and Kush, what is known is that Rome placed heavy taxation rates on the Nubian kingdom, demanding goods and services in an attempt to make Kush a client kingdom.[107]

Soon after the negotiations in 24 BCE, Kandake Amanirenas led an army of thirty thousand warriors and pushed as far into Egypt as the First Cataract at Aswan, overwhelming the city and taking its statues into their possession. Choosing not to occupy Aswan and Philae due to being so far from her supply lines, Amanirenas wisely pulled her armies back into Nubian territory, conducting regular raids along Egypt's southern border. Publius Petronius, the Roman governor of Egypt, ordered swift retaliation, sending ten thousand infantry and cavalry units deep into Kushite territory to brutally sack the sacred city of Napata, toppling its famed Temple of Amun and razing much of the city to the ground. The Roman army took the people of Napata as slaves, even sending one thousand of them to the emperor to use in the games and setting up a military garrison to use

---

[106] Mark, Joshua. (2018). "The Candaces of Meroe." World History.org. 30 July 2021. https://www.worldhistory.org/The_Candaces_of_Meroe/.

[107] Welsby, Derek A. (1996). *The Kingdom of Kush*. British Museum Press. p 64-65.

as a forward operations base for an intended invasion of Upper Nubia.

However, while Rome thought a blatant show of force would make Kush cower, they had extremely underestimated the queen of Meroe. Passionately rousing her military, Kandake Amanirenas again marched north to attack the cliff-top city of Qasr Ibrim, Rome's primary defensive outpost that protected Aswan.[108] Petronius's scouts, however, alerted the governor of Amanirenas's army's advance.

Knowing that Aswan's defenses were not enough to prevent a complete Kushite invasion of southern Egypt, Petronius marched his army south, sending his engineers in advance to fortify Qasr Ibrim's walls. Upon her arrival, Amanirenas ordered a brutal attack on the fortress, decimating its defenses with her archers before sending an initial wave of her infantry to engage Rome's recently arrived forces. Knowing Petronius was in no position to hold the fortress and thus stop a Nubian invasion of southern Egypt, Kandake Amanirenas

---

[108] Jackson, Robert B. (2002). *At Empire's Edge: Exploring Rome's Egyptian Frontier*. Yale University Press.

dispatched emissaries to negotiate peace settlements with the governor.[109]

With an accord reached, establishing favorable trade conditions between Rome and Nubia and a hard border at Maharraqa, 130 miles south of Aswan, Amanirenas withdrew her forces to nearby Abu Simbel. As part of the peace treaty, Amanirenas's ambassadors were to return the regal statuary that was seized during Kush's initial raids into Aswan. It was the Romans' custom when taking new territory to place statues of Augustus Caesar in temples and government buildings in order to demonstrate to the newly conquered people who their new ruler was. In taking the statuary, Kush was, in effect, removing the physical symbol of Egypt's ruling authority. Amanirenas obliged the Roman governor in his request, returning the statuary to Aswan. However, the largest statue of Augustus Caesar was returned with its head missing. The Nubians claimed that the head had been hacked off during the assault and lost in the return march. However, in 1910, the massive bronze head of the emperor was discovered buried under a staircase leading into the Temple of Amun in Meroe during an archaeological expedition.[110] Amanirenas had the sculpture buried underneath the temple walkway, which presumably led to an altar marking Kush's victory at Aswan, so that the people of Meroe would walk upon the head of the Roman emperor every day.

The peace agreement between Kush and Rome would last for over three hundred years, lasting until the eventual fall of Meroe in the 4th century. While small skirmishes were common, they were generally taken care of by local authorities, who were empowered by the kings and queens of Kush to maintain peace. Trade between Rome and Kush was profitable for both governments, with Meroe developing blast furnaces for the quick production of iron used in weapons and

---

[109] Robinson, Arthur. (1928). "The Arab Dynasty of Dar For (Darfur): Part II." *Journal of the Royal African Society London Vol. XXVIII.* p 55-67.

[110] MacGregor, Neil. (2013). *A History of the World in 100 Objects.* Penguin Books.

tools, as well as being Rome's source for trade goods, agricultural goods, and slaves.[111]

Between the 1st and 4th century CE, the kings and queens of Kush would subdivide Nubia into territories, with generals overseeing their administration. However, in decentralizing their government, a number of these generals began to act as warlords, hiring mercenary armies from the Eastern Desert to extend their kingdoms. Between the decentralization of its power and the deforestation of Nubia due to stripping the forests for fuel for iron production, Meroe's trade power began to dip significantly. In the south, the stable Kingdom of Aksum began to take Kush's place as Roman Egypt's primary trade partner in northeast Africa.

Vulnerable and unable to maintain control over its own empire, Meroe was invaded by King Ezana of Aksum in circa 340 CE, crushing the city and taking its people into slavery.[112] By 350, the once-powerful city of Meroe was left in shambles, its infrastructure destroyed, its glory vanished.

With the fall of Meroe, the empire of Kush crumbled. Territorial governors would continue to squabble for power and crumbs over the next century, but their memory and monuments would, for the most part, be lost. Following the fracturing of the Kushite empire, a people known as the Nobatae, also known as the Ballana culture, began a gradual takeover of southern Kush's former cities and villages, establishing small kingdoms. King Silko would eventually unite these kingdoms into the Kingdom of Nobatia and would become the first Christian ruler of ancient Nubia, effectively ending the Kushite empire by moving on from its culture and religion. The Kush empire was left to be hidden by the shifting desert sands, its majesty forgotten for almost two thousand years.

---

[111] Welsby, Derek. (1996). *The Kingdom of Kush*. British Museum Press. p 64–65.

[112] Munro-Hay, S.C. (1991). *Aksum: An African Civilization of Late Antiquity*. Edinburgh: University Press. p. 81.

Chapter 6 – The Pyramids of Ancient Nubia

A short book on ancient Nubia would not be complete without a more detailed examination of its pyramids. Rising to one hundred feet into the air, the Sudanese pyramids dominate the barren landscape around them, enticing the mind to come alive with visions of how they appeared in the past and what they can tell us about those who built them. Modern-day Sudan is home to the largest collection of pyramids in the world, but due to regional economic conditions, environmental factors, and frequent wars, Nubia's ancient pyramids are rarely visited or investigated.

Unlike many of their similar cousins in Egypt, the Nubian pyramids are grouped in clusters, with one site at Meroe containing more pyramids than in all of Egypt. These pyramids, which point like arrowheads sprouting from the desert sands, stand in now desolate areas such as El-Kurru and Jebel Barkal, marking the former grandeur of long-forgotten kingdoms, kings, queens, and nobility.

After being conquered by the Egyptians during the New Kingdom, the Nubians lived under the rule of the pharaoh for over five hundred years. But as you have seen, Nubia and Egypt did not have a simple relationship. The Nubian kingdoms and the empires of Egypt interacted with and rivaled each other over thousands of years, influencing one another in an epic dance of give and take. As the Kingdom of Kush rose, Nubian pharaohs served on the Egyptian throne. And as Kush fell, the kingdoms of Nubia were consolidated at the city of Meroe. The Nubians worshiped the same gods as the Egyptians, employed several of the same religious burial customs, and even gave the Egyptian god Amun precedence over local gods. The Nubian pyramids are a part of this dance of intermingling cultures, bearing traces of Egyptian inspiration, but at their hearts, they thoroughly belong to Nubia.

The first Nubian pyramid is believed to have been constructed circa 700 BCE, 1,800 years after the construction of the Great Pyramid of Cheops and 800 years after the *last* royal pyramid of Egypt was constructed by Ahmose I. While Egypt abandoned the pyramid design almost one thousand years earlier, Nubian architects took the pyramid design of Egypt and improved upon it, building them more efficiently and more durable. While many of Egypt's smaller pyramids have crumbled to dust, most of Nubia's ancient pyramids still stand.

Nubian pyramids are noticeably smaller than their Egyptian counterparts. While the Great Pyramid reaches 430 feet into the sky (and was the world's tallest building for over 4,000 years), the tallest Nubian pyramid is 98 feet tall. However, it is for this reason that so many Nubian pyramids still exist.

Egyptian pyramids are theorized to have been designed by pushing blocks up long slopes using multiple series of counterweights, balances, and wet sand. The construction of Egyptian pyramids was a massive endeavor, utilizing enormous amounts of man-hours and planning. Thus, they were incredible drains on the coffers of the treasury. Estimates suggest that if the Great Pyramid was built today, it would cost more than five *billion* dollars to construct.[113] Large bricks weighing two thousand to five thousand pounds were often used in their construction and were often filled with shafts leading to tombs or theorized ceremonial areas.

Nubian pyramids, however, were built using a mechanism called a shadoof. A Nubian shadoof is a simple counterpoise lift, and it is still used to irrigate farms today and is popular across the world. Used in Nubia since approximately 2000 BCE, shadoofs were originally designed to lift water from rivers or wells and then drop the water via

---

[113] Wolchover, Natalie. (2012). "How Much Would it Cost to Build the Great Pyramid Today?" LIVE SCIENCE. 28 July 2021. https://www.livescience.com/18589-cost-build-great-pyramid-today.html.

a bucket into nearby water basins or channels to direct the water elsewhere. The shadoof is easy to construct, and it is made from an upright frame and a long pole leaning against it. At the top of the pole hangs a bucket or large skin. At the bottom of the pole is a weight, which serves as a counterpoise. The operator, using their own weight, can effortlessly push the pole down to effectively lower the long end, and the weight lifts it back up, depositing the water into buckets or channels that move the water toward its intended purpose. When shadoofs are used to move water, studies in Sudan and Chad have shown that when lifting water from rivers or nearby water sources, one man can move up to 10 to 37 gallons per minute.[114]

Nubian engineers realized that in improving upon the model of the simple shadoof, they could use it to quickly move large blocks of sandstone and granite. Using a strengthened shadoof that acted as a crane, Nubian engineers would select the site of the pyramid (some theorize to match the pattern of certain constellations in the sky, set the crane, and then build the pyramid around it.[115, 116] This is the explanation for the narrower base of Sudanese pyramids, as a shadoof can only lift blocks the length of four-fifths of the pole, as one-fifth of the pole must be reserved for the counterweight. Once the height of the blocks made the interior position of the shadoof untenable, the shadoof would be disassembled, the interior would be filled with a mixture of stone and packed sand, and then the upper blocks would be swung into position by shadoofs erected on the outside. Once the blocks were moved into place, polished granite and sandstone blocks were used on the outside to give the pyramids a smooth surface

---

[114] *Shaduf Project*. (2004). SHADUF Project. 28 July 2021. http://www.shaduf-eu.org/.

[115] MacDonald, James. (2015). *The Forgotten Pyramids of Sudan*. JSTOR Daily. 28 July 2021. https://daily.jstor.org/forgotten-pyramids-sudan/.

[116] Budge, Wallace, E. (1899). "The Orientation of the Pyramids and Temples of the Sudan." *Proceedings of the Royal Society of London, Vol 65*. p 333-349.

inclined at seventy degrees, whereas most Egyptian pyramids were inclined between forty-two to fifty-one degrees.

Once the pyramid was constructed, most Nubian pyramids would have an offering temple built next to them. It was in these temples that Nubians would leave offerings for the departed to use in the afterlife or offer prayers. These offering temples are usually small spaces measuring less than ten feet by ten feet, but they are a treasure trove for archaeologists, as they are often filled with wall carvings depicting daily life for the ancients: queens or kings ruling their people, priests and nobility performing their sacred duties, and more.

Most pyramids are believed to have been built by Kushite rulers and nobility. The first pyramids were built at El-Kurru and mimicked the pyramid styles of Egypt's New Kingdom period with attached temples. The first Nubian pyramids were built to honor King Kashta and King Piye. Subsequent pyramids were built for other Nubian pharaohs: Shabaka (Shabaqo), Shebitku (Shabataka), and then Tantamani. These kings had additional pyramids designed for their warrior queens.

At Nuri, six miles north from El-Kurru along the Nile, another necropolis was constructed for King Taharqa. Along with his large pyramid that measured almost 150 feet high, this complex would eventually grow to house over 20 kings, 52 queens, and numerous princes and princesses. These tombs differed slightly from the earlier designs at El-Kurru, as they feature burial chambers underneath that contained sarcophagi that weighed over 15 tons.[117]

The necropolis of Meroe, however, is the crown jewel of Nubia's ancient pyramid group. Located south between the Nile's Fifth and Sixth Cataracts, more pyramids are contained within Meroe than within all of Egypt. Containing the monuments of over forty queens and kings, Meroe's necropolis is also filled with the elite of Meroitic society, including what are believed to be wealthy commoners and tradesmen.

---

[117] Lehner, Mark. (1997). *The Complete Pyramids*. Thames and Hudson. p 196-197.

While most burial chambers underneath the pyramids of Nubia demonstrate evidence of being plundered, a number have revealed their secrets to archaeologists. Bows and arrows, weapons, poison-tipped arrows, thumb rings of archers, boxes, furniture, pottery, polished faience, metal plates and pourers, and various other discovered items have revealed the prized possessions of daily life in ancient Nubia, as well as the extensive trade between Egypt and other Mediterranean countries. One chamber even revealed an entire cow that had been buried with its owner, as well as stones that, when tapped with sticks, create musical notes.[118]

Believed to hold immense wealth, the pyramids of Nubia were frequent targets of tomb raiders. The most famous (and despised) treasure hunter of Sudan's pyramids was Giuseppe Ferlini, an Italian soldier who, in the 1830s, blew up over forty Nubian pyramids using high-charged explosives while searching for gold. Finding silver and gold underneath only one pyramid, he took his ill-gotten gains to Europe to attempt to sell them. In order to hide his discovery from

---

[118] The Great Green Wall. (2021). "The Great Green Wall." 28 July 2021. https://www.greatgreenwall.org/about-great-green-wall.

other plunderers, Ferlini also blew up the tops of other pyramids so they would not know where to search for treasure. However, as most historians believed that Sudan at the time of the Egyptians was a backwater and primitive area, Ferlini had difficulty selling his plundered treasure. Eventually, King Ludwig I of Bavaria purchased some of the Sudanese treasure, which is now housed in the State Museum of Egyptian Art in Munich, with the remainder housed in the Egyptian Museum of Berlin.[119] Other tomb raiders would follow the terrible example of Ferlini and use explosive charges on the tops of pyramids before the practice was abandoned in the late 1800s. This has led to what appear to be fields of broken arrowheads along the desert sands.

In 1897, a major expedition was put together to excavate several Nubian pyramids at Jebel Barkal. The British excavators, believing that the interior of the Nubian pyramids was similar to that of Egyptian ones, were surprised to find that Nubian pyramids were completely solid on the inside with no chambers. Realizing that the Nubian pyramids were, in essence, giant headstones, British investigators concluded that the burial chambers lay beneath the pyramids. A number of these pyramids, such as King Nastasen's Pyramid and King Taharqa's Pyramid at the complex at Nuri, are now

---

[119] Welsby, Derek A. (1998). *The Kingdom of Kush: The Napatan and Meroitic Empire*. Princeton, New Jersey: Markus Wiener. p 86, 185.

filled with rising groundwater, preventing investigation until only recently by underwater archaeologists.[120]

Granted UNESCO World Heritage status in 2011, the pyramids of ancient Nubia stand as silent sentinels in the desert sands, harkening back to a time when the remnants of grasslands and fertile fields swept the region and metropolitan cities dotted the landscape along the Nile. Lasting thousands of years, the Sudanese pyramids are now at risk from ever-increasing harsh weather and sandstorms due to climate change. Overwhelming evidence suggests that changing temperatures have made the land more arid, increasing the rate and power of sandstorms so that they can engulf houses and buildings within moments, erasing carvings and stonework with their ferocity.[121]

Archaeologists and climatologists are moving quickly to both preserve and protect the precious monuments of a nearly lost culture with projects such as the Great Green Wall, but it may already be too late.[122] The secrets of ancient Nubia and its pyramids are at great risk of being lost forever, sunk beneath the desert sands and rising groundwater tables of Sudan.

---

[120] Romey, Kristin. (2019). "Dive Beneath the Pyramids of Sudan's Black Pharaohs." National Geographic. 28 July 2021. https://www.nationalgeographic.com/culture/article/dive-ancient-pyramid-nuri-sudan.

[121] de Freitas, Will. (2021). "Sudan's 'forgotten' pyramids risk being buried by shifting sand dunes." The Conversation. 28 July 2021. https://theconversation.com/sudans-forgotten-pyramids-risk-being-buried-by-shifting-sand-dunes-159596.

[122] The Great Green Wall. (2021). "The Great Green Wall." 28 July 2021. https://www.greatgreenwall.org/about-great-green-wall.

Conclusion – The Mystery in the Sands

The incredible power and wealth of the kingdoms and empires of ancient Nubia carved a significant place into some of the greatest empires in the history of the world. Its impact upon the cultures of the world's mightiest kingdoms should place Nubia's achievements into the same conversations as that of Egypt and other powers of the Mediterranean.

But for a civilization responsible for so much, why is so little known about ancient Nubia? Why is the landscape of ancient Nubia not swarmed with archaeological digs and excavations like its neighbor to the north? And why has modern archaeology shied away from the powerful influence of ancient Nubia upon Egyptian culture and trade throughout the Mediterranean?

Why has the modern mind forgotten such an important culture, whose very existence made so much of Mediterranean and African culture possible?

For a culture so vital to so many of the civilizations of the ancient world, why do the secrets of ancient Nubia still lie beneath swirling desert sands?

While the answers are not simple, there are many theories why Nubia is not mentioned in the same breath as that of Egypt.

The first is the absence of understood written languages, and we can look no further than Egypt to the north to understand why. Much of our knowledge of Egyptian culture was lost and rarely discussed until the discovery of the Rosetta Stone in 1799 by French soldiers in Napoleon Bonaparte's army. When it was deciphered in the early 19th century by scholars, the infatuation with Egypt began, as historians could now understand what was hidden in the Egyptian sands. Much of our knowledge of Nubia comes from Egyptian sources, and since ancient Nubia was often Egypt's primary competition throughout its existence, Egypt typically painted the empires of Nubia in a negative light.

The second reason, and one that is oft-debated in our present culture, is much more insidious. When Giuseppe Ferlini destroyed the pyramids of Nubia in his search for fame and fortune, he ran into difficulties selling his goods in Egypt because the majority of European buyers did not believe that ancient Nubians could produce such magnificent works. In the 1800s, the Egyptians were believed to have been Mediterranean and Middle-Eastern skinned, and the

Nubians were of a darker color, as depicted upon tombs and papyri. Kush was associated with "black Africa," and therefore, it was primitive. During Reisner's excavations of Meroe and then Lower Nubia, he wrongly assumed that Kushite leaders were like their Egyptian neighbors to the north and were Mediterranean and Middle-Eastern skinned. He could not believe that sub-Saharan Africans were capable of building such incredible monuments and glorious kingdoms, and he even went as far as to claim that "the ignorant black population were elevated by their monarchs exposing them to Egyptian culture."[123] The same could be said in regard to Kush's powerful female rulers. It has not been believed until recently that Kandakes were capable of ruling without serving as co-regents. Our terrible biases have discounted so much of Nubia's achievements due to ridiculous assumptions based upon horrid views on race and gender.

Biases aside, the kingdoms of ancient Nubia altered the course of world history throughout its six-thousand-year existence, and their influence was felt as far away as India and China. And this was before the days of airplane travel and satellite internet.

And Nubia's mysteries are still locked beneath the sands of the brutal deserts of Sudan. If any excitement can be taken from overcoming terrible biases, it is that so much of Nubia's magnificence is still waiting to be discovered. Nubia's own Rosetta Stone is out there. It must be. And it is waiting to be found.

Nubia's ancient knowledge waits to be discovered, waiting for its glory to be revealed to the world. Maybe the answers to its riddles sit silently in its forgotten tombs, waiting for the right time for the world to fully embrace their revelation.

Maybe that time is now. And maybe, just maybe, the one who solves its riddles might be you.

---

[123] Mark, Joshua. (2018). "The Candaces of Meroe." World History.org. 30 July 2021. https://www.worldhistory.org/The_Candaces_of_Meroe/.

Free Bonus from Captivating History (Available for a Limited time)

Hi History Lovers!

Now you have a chance to join our exclusive history list so you can get your first history ebook for free as well as discounts and a potential to get more history books for free! Simply visit the link below to join.

Captivatinghistory.com/ebook

Also, make sure to follow us on Facebook, Twitter and Youtube by searching for Captivating History.

Here's another book by Captivating History that you might like

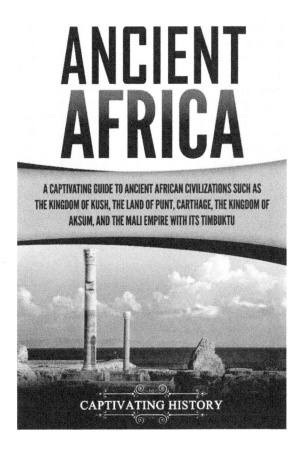

Made in the USA
Monee, IL
19 April 2022